Losing Your Mind

Losing Your Mind

Beyond Heaven
Past the Light
Something Waits

Karen Alexander
Rick Boyes

Boise, Idaho

Losing Your Mind
Beyond Heaven
Past The Light
Something Waits

© 1995 Windover Press

Published by:
Windover Press
967 E. Parkcenter Boulevard, Suite 306
Boise, ID 83706-6700
(208) 388-0180

94-061566
ISBN 1-885733-24-0 : $14.95
Cover design and typography by Vicki Marsh

Second printing,
Printed in the U.S.A.
on acid-free recycled paper

for Daniel

Prologue

Falling now, radiant love, its
spinning threads of light
compelled from the darkness.
Fed by endless fountains of
delight, sent forth with all
that is needed, you are never
alone, never forgotten and
always, there is a whisper,
my encouragement, my
gratitude.

You are my creation, my thought,
my heart, and into you I pour
all of my hope, forever and ever.
For it is you who will bring
what I need to take us both
home. And all around us,

sparkling particle by particle,
others spin in the darkness
and light comes into form.
And they are filled then with
purpose and infinite love even as
Gaia's body and boundless love
brings forth all her creatures.

And when it is time, I will call
you back into myself and receive
from you the treasure you hold.
I will embrace you even as I do
now and there you will hear
again all the love of the soul
and feel again the caress of my
hand and gather my tears of
joy and dissolve into my heart,
one forever with all that is.

And I sing to you my precious
creation, my perfect minion.
Take from me your life and all
my courage, receive from me all
of what you will need and do

for me what I wish. For your deepest desire is what I also long for. Together, joined and blended, dancing light to light, we will leave the darkness forever behind and enter into the union from which we came.

Do not be afraid, for as much as the heart beats now in your chest, as much as the air flows into your body, so I am with you always. And lift up not your eyes and ears, for these are only needed to make your way in your earthtime explorations. But free the strands of light which make your heart and reach these up into the darkness. There in the stillness, you will feel my touch and then entwined, you will fill with me and know me. And there will be no end, for there is no separation but that which is made by confusion and ignorance.

And sing without ceasing to our sister Gaia as her gentle lullaby comforts you, as her creations nourish your sojourn in the earthtime. For it is forever a circle of love ... it always has been ... and always will be.

Come, come my cherished creation, come into your purpose, come into alignment, come into knowing who you are ... and from this place, never be alone, never be again lost in the darkness. Falling now, glorious spinning light, filled with love, birthed into being ... you are forever and ever mine.

Chapter 1

Barely seat-back high, the bobbing spray of blond hair moved slowly toward me down the aisle. Everything went into slow motion as the flight attendant bent over, read his ticket and turned toward me. I tried to look away, but with radar accuracy, she had already locked on. Her left arm rose and straightened, the index finger extending its deadly aim. Without sympathy, she pronounced my sentence, "Right there next to that man." With the sensation of teeth biting into aluminum foil, the words met my mind and the muscles in the back of my neck agreed to permanent gridlock.

Why me? I had been within a breath of having an empty seat next to me for the entire transatlantic flight. Now, I was condemned to eleven hours strapped next to a seven year old. That's forty-eight years in grown up time. I wondered how I could stay clear of an endless conversation with this little kid.

"Can I sit by the window?" he asked sweetly.

"No!" I blurted. Then, uncomfortable with my own rudeness, I looked over to astonishing eyes. Like the shallow water in a peaceful lagoon somewhere warm and beautiful, they were clear blue. Set in a whimsical face, translucent white skin glowing under the wayward blond hair, those eyes were still, calm and peaceful.

As I gazed at him, I felt embarrassed about my behavior and decided to recant my former edict. "You can have the window seat. Nothing out there to see on this flight anyway."

"That's the best time to look," he replied, his seven-year old voice containing an enthusiasm suited to flying straight over Disneyland.

Strange kid, I thought. He'll probably talk non-stop, incessantly commenting on everything and anything, an endless source of useless noise, the

1

kind with enough variety you can't ever get used to it to the point of blocking it out.

My friends have children like this. They have provided me with a colorful collection of reasons never to have children. I like children, other people's children, in other people's homes for very short periods of time with absolutely nothing blocking the door when I decide it's time for me to go. And don't leave me alone with any of them. Nearly every conversation I've ever had with a child goes like this:

"Hi. What's your name?"

Silence.

"How old are you?"

Silence.

"Do you go to school?"

Silence.

"Do you like school?"

Silence.

This effort is always followed by an interminable period while the child continues to look at me, still silently, but with a new unspoken judgment and edge of pity because I cannot for the life of me figure out anything else to say. When his mother or father finally returns, my heart surges, suddenly full of gratitude normally reserved for being rescued at sea after ten days without food or water.

Then the noise starts. With a mysterious invisible "on switch" tripped magically by a parent entering the room, this silent sphinx bursts to life at volume ten. Suddenly, he cannot stop talking and jumps up and down without a clue about social distance. Feeling like the target of a hysterical cat, I try to release myself from the confusion of arms and legs grabbing at my body. I need to back up for a minute, develop a plan, decide what to do. Not possible. The child gathers reinforcements. Toys with names and purposes I've never heard of, and explanations in fragments that sound like what comes out of a radio when the dial is turned too fast.

The little voice broke through my ruminations, "My name is Daniel." Guileless eyes were fixed upon my face, waiting for an answer.

Here we go, I thought. The beginning of eleven hours of unwanted interaction. "I'm Rick," I said quietly.

"Yep, you are." He offered this curious statement with an element of appreciation in his voice. I caught myself looking at this little boy wearing a bright blue t-shirt tucked neatly into gray sweatpants. His hightop sneakers looked well-used, and now clacked together with a syncopated rhythm that meant something only to him.

Our plane's engines began to whine like a massive choir of insects and we moved slowly backwards. A surge of responsibility came up within me, "Put your seat belt on." I couldn't really just ignore him all the way to London.

We sat at the end of the runway and it seemed impossible this massive collection of technology could ever make it off the ground. I thought about a friend who told me these planes get into the air through the efforts of tiny, invisible, tribal strongmen; she called them "menehunes." Supposedly, they raced along beneath the wings, bare feet pounding in powerful unison. At precisely the right instant, they would vault the giant mechanical beast into the sky. On every flight since she told me that story, I checked for them with one eye.

Maybe I should tell the kid about the menehunes. I was willing to talk to him while we took off, even hold his hand if he wanted me to. "Are you scared about flying?" I asked.

"I like to fly," he answered brightly. "I fly all the time."

"By yourself?" I questioned. He seemed so young to be traveling alone.

"Yep," he nodded. "Well, nobody's ever really by themselves."

He's a confident little kid, I thought. Maybe one parent lives in the States and the other in London.

"How many times have you flown to London?" I inquired.

"A bunch of times, and all over other places too," he answered with a smile.

"How come you get to travel so much?" I asked, feeling a little envious. I loved to travel, but except for a few trips to the Oregon coast, I was seventeen years old before I really left Idaho.

He responded with positive certainty, "Everybody can travel all over if they really want to."

That's it, I decided, he must be an airlines kid. He can fly anywhere and thinks everyone can do it.

We were in the air! Finally, I was on my way to London. Feeling excited and relieved, I began mentally to organize the flight. I had an excellent book, they were showing a good movie. There was always music on the headphones, food, a nap, more food. . .

It was good to leave work behind, even for a few days. If I allowed myself to get tired enough, I began to feel maybe the critics were right. Maybe psychotherapy couldn't really help anybody after all. I had certainly chalked up my share of success stories and most of my new clients were coming from word of mouth, a good sign, but still there was a certain dissatisfaction with my work.

I was adept at discovering the dynamics creating a client's symptoms. Invariably, she would be quite impressed with these new cognitive insights into why she was depressed, anxious, had panic attacks, drank too much, couldn't sleep or kept getting involved in the same dysfunctional relationship patterns over and over again. For a few sessions we would bask in the afterglow of these new revelations and the client would lavish me with praise for being such a great therapist.

But, the glamour would fade as we sat there and realized, although she now understood perfectly why her life had been plagued with such symptoms, she still got depressed, felt anxious, had to fight off the panic attacks, drank too much, tossed and turned all night and continued to accept dinner invitations from guys who were making alimony payments in six states. In the vast majority of cases, there seemed to be very little correlation between a client's intellectual understanding and anything really changing on the emotional level.

This was especially true in the most complex cases. I wanted to do something more for those individuals who had suffered through a lifetime of mental anguish and had seen more therapists than could be counted. I was touched by those whose eyes no longer held any light of hope. I didn't want to be just another shrink with another line, but my energy could not overcome the inertia of thirty years of pain that went soul deep.

There had to be a better way. I could not bring myself to accept that certain individuals were destined to be permanently trapped in a private hell. People were being medicated at an alarming rate and an artificial abatement of symptoms seemed to be accepted as an appropriate therapeutic goal. But, I clung to the belief recovery was not the psychological equivalent of growing a third arm. Surely, these suffering clients were not trying to do something against the natural order of life itself.

After several years of practicing traditional therapy, I went to Los Angeles and studied clinical hypnotherapy. Profoundly impressed, I learned analytical hypnotherapy techniques which cut right to the emotional core of the problem. This was not simply a bandaid for symptoms, but a powerful and deep resolution of issues at a profoundly deep level. People were not abandoned to continue their suffering with only an intellectual grasp of the underlying dynamics of their symptoms. Real change had taken place! Why had this information not been presented to me in my University studies? Why was there not a single program in the country leading to a degree in psychology or psychiatry that required training in hypnotherapy?

I had taken my new found skills home, and with the excitement and energy generated from hope, set out to help those clients whose emotional problems had not responded to other forms of treatment. Soon, I was inundated with difficult cases. My days were filled with clients who had survived the most terrible forms of childhood abuse, whose lives were spent literally trying to make it from one minute to the next. Often, their stories included experiences with tremendously inept counselors and physicians. Sadly, my belief that the mental health system of our country was in dismal shape continued to grow.

Many of these clients experienced dramatic improvement with the use of hypnotherapy. And yet, there were still some who were caught in a web of pain. Every counselor has a few clients who only want an uninterrupted opportunity to tell another human being how awful life is. But others were not professional complainers. They desperately wanted things to change and yet, despite our greatest efforts, their suffering continued. I knew the human psyche contained an element that will push for growth and happiness with the intensity of a river cutting through a mountain to reach the ocean. How could that be unleashed? What might be affecting the human condition I had no idea about?

"Flying on an airplane sure takes a long time." The young voice broke into my painful thoughts.

"Yes, sometimes it does," I responded patiently. "We're flying all the way to the other side of the world and that's a long way. You know that, Daniel. You said you've flown to London lots of times."

He really was kind of cute. Face pressed up against the window, he seemed completely engrossed in watching the clouds underneath us. Maybe this flight wouldn't be so bad, after all. I opened my book.

"Rick," the soft voice found me once again. "Do you want to see some of the places I can go?" I glanced up to find eyes alert with expectation.

I supposed he had family travel pictures to show me. I was curious to see where he had visited. "O.K. Daniel, let's take a look at what you've got."

Releasing the seat belt, he wiggled himself down onto the floor. Wedged up against my leg, his little back strained to pull out a bright red backpack stashed under the seat ahead of him.

"Need some help?" I said, reaching down for his bag.

Like a fisherman with an enormous catch on the line, he tugged away at his prize. "No, I can get it," he answered. Finally, he released a big breath and pushed the bag up onto his seat.

"Do you want to see?" he asked, looking straight up at me.

"Sure, why not?" I said good naturedly.

"Do you want to see?" he repeated, strangely serious in his persistence.

"Yes, Yes, I said Yes." Everything is always such a production with kids. When I thought about it, that was what bugged me about them.

"Rick, you have to want to see," he said gently. Somehow, the little voice slipped inside me and snared my mind. Sparkling blue eyes locked with mine and the small hand reached out and touched my face. A sensation of overwhelming love coursed through me. It was an odd sort of love, more like an unbearable compassion combined with great joy.

Lost for a moment in the exquisite rush of feeling, I closed my eyes and allowed myself to receive it. I was floating, drifting on the river in the summertime of my childhood. Settled into an inner tube, hot sun on my legs and cool water falling in a slow motion, a glittering collection of tiny drops, suspended in the sunshine, I was in heaven.

Love, how desperate we are to receive it, find it, experience it, trap it and own it. And once done, it so quickly dies inside its cage of expectations and failed dreams. How angry we are when it cannot survive its imprisonment. Attacking, we tear it into a thousand pieces and judge each one into oblivion. Then we grieve. What we needed most has died at our own hands. Soon, we begin the hunt for this elusive requirement for survival. But, this was wonderful, so innocent, so clearly beyond containment.

Abruptly, energy shot through my body and the astounding peace was replaced by a fervor, a passion. Like an electrical current surging up from my feet through my legs and urgently moving without restraint, this power inside insisted its way into my chest, entered my heart and erupted in a celebration of feelings I did not know I could have. My eyes sprung open

6

to find the child who had brought me to such a place within myself. The blue eyes were there, filled now with amusement.

The plane was gone.

Chapter 2

In the distance, I could just see the high, white tail of the 747 disappear into a bank of soft, gray clouds. My mind buckled like a piece of cardboard held up to a strong wind. Instinctively, I began pumping my arms and legs wildly, flapping like a strange, spasmodic bird.

The plane's gone! It's not here! The voice inside my head screamed like a heavy metal singer into his microphone. Think. Think. Think. Think. I'm going to die. The plane's gone. What do you mean, think? The goddamn plane is gone. I'm going to fall. I'm going to die.

Past the frantic frenzy of my arms, I saw the little boy. Peacefully standing there, he said quietly, "You don't need to do that. Everything's O.K."

I was shouting in terror, "Everything's O.K.?! The plane's gone. There. . . is. . . no. . . plane. We've lost everything. We're going to fall!" Think. Think. Think. There is no plane and I'm trying to convince a seven year old that it's important!

"Look around," he said with the amusement now in his voice. "Are we falling?"

A wailing noise came from my mouth, "Of course we're falling. There is no plane. Without the plane, we fall. . ."

"Rick, are we falling?" The little voice was so quiet, so comfortable.

I made myself look down and saw gray mist, shifting silently across my legs and feet. I wasn't going anywhere, not down, not up, not anywhere at all. My head whipped up in astonishment. "What the hell is going on here?"

The little boy giggled, his face demonstrating a child's honesty at seeing something he finds absolutely hysterical. His musical laughter filled the silence and I felt the mist surround my body and play across my face.

8

Gratefully, I took in that beautiful fragrance of raindrops early in the morning.

I loved playing in the rain. Big red rubber boots on my feet, I'd jump in every puddle I could find and laugh and laugh, even when the mud would splash up and cover my clothes and I knew my mom would be mad. The harder it rained, the happier I'd get. Our neighbor, Mr. Henderson, would finally yell past his screen door, "Boy! Don't you know enough to get out of the rain?" I did, and I knew I needed to stay out in the rain.

Somehow, the rain replenished my soul. In some mysterious way, it fed me deep down inside. Everything would seem new, the trees, my neighborhood, my house, even me. Cleansed, free, clear, we all had a new start. I'd come in only when some adult would finally find it necessary to intrude on my bliss. Even after the obligatory hot bath, insisted upon by my mother to save me from an undefined, but terrible illness, I would stand by the window and watch the raindrops pass by the street light on their way to the earth and wonder who had sent them.

"Are you coming?" Daniel had stopped giggling and looked at me intently.

"What?" I managed to choke out. My body was no longer fighting to prevent a fall. But, go somewhere? My mind fought to find an explanation for what was happening and came to an obvious conclusion. This had to be an absolutely terrifying dream.

Wake up! This is one of those awful falling dreams where you topple from a building and wake up just before you hit the pavement. Everyone has dreams like that. Just like the one where you look down and find yourself naked in a restaurant or the one that has the phone that won't work in an emergency. Regular, bad dreams. This was a complex one of those. O.K. Wake up!

"Are you coming?" Daniel spoke again. God, he seemed so real. And the taste of the clouds. So real. . . wake up!

"You said you wanted to see where I can go. . ." The little boy voice fed back my statement with a kind of positive neutrality, just a fact to be gently reminded of.

"O.K. Daniel, I don't understand what's happening here." God, I'm talking to a hallucination. That's it, some sort of horrible drug had gotten into my system. How could that happen? I don't take drugs. I missed the 60's. I have never taken drugs.

Daniel spoke again, "Rick, it's either important or it's not. You have to decide. . . are you coming?" He turned and started to move away. Hallucination or not, I didn't want to be left alone.

"O.K., O.K. I'll come," I sputtered.

The most beautiful smile I had ever seen changed the little face into a beacon of joy; he was so happy. Actually, he was ecstatic. "That's good," was all he said, but it felt like a blessing.

Somewhere, I had heard the best thing to do with a bad trip was to try to relax and not fight it. If you accept you're helplessly along for the ride, it would be a lot easier. In six, eight hours it will be over. Then, I could get off the plane in London, go to a good hotel, eat, rest, call somebody, and forget this bizarre thing ever happened to me.

"Daniel." I tried to steady myself. "Daniel, where are we going? How are we going to get there?"

The joyful smile still on his face, he replied softly, "It's easy, all you have to do is remember who you are."

"Who am I?" I've been trying to figure that out my whole life.

I guess it starts in school. "Who you are" gets translated to "What can you do?" From the blue bird vs. the red bird reading groups in the first grade, the entire system is set up to reveal who is competent and skilled and who is not.

Who learns to tell time first? Who has the best spelling test? Who can add and subtract better than anyone else? There are layers and layers of this method of classifying human beings. Who can run faster and climb higher, who hits the ball every time? Who is prettiest? Who has the nicest clothes, the best smile? Which child is most cooperative and pleasant, and which seems destined to lead?

Kids arrive at school with family beliefs well-entrenched: "You're just like your uncle Fred." "Everyone in our family has always been good at this." "A Smith doesn't think like that." "Honey, you won't ever be good at math." "Don't waste your time like that, let me show you how it's done." "People in Boise don't act that way." "You're the kind of kid that will grow up to be a teacher."

I spent a lot of time helping my clients break free of the things they had learned about themselves which were untrue, or simply no longer applicable. I strongly believed most things could be changed with a determined willingness to do the work. But who did the person really start out to become? That was a difficult question.

I climbed out of my thoughts as Daniel said quite seriously, "Rick, you must remember who you are."

I didn't know what he wanted from me. "O.K. I am Rick." That sounded silly. Of course, I could remember my name. What was the point?

"Well. . ." Mist drifted past the little hallucination's face and I impatiently waited for him to explain. "Rick is the name of your body and the name of what you do, but that's not who you are."

Feeling agitated with this convoluted answer to a question I did not even understand, I asked irritably, "Daniel, just what do you mean?" I was ready to leave this dream world. I wanted the trip to be over. I'd had enough. Daniel's eyes danced with a loving humor that only increased my aggravation.

"Just tell me what you mean or help me get out of here." There, I had asked the product of my drugged state to help me out of the drugged state. That was scary.

"You haven't been drugged, you know." He looked at me with renewed intensity.

How did he do that? "I didn't say anything, how did you know what I was thinking?"

"It's easy," he replied with a grin. "You just have to remember who it is that you really are."

"I give up." How was I going to figure out what he wanted from me? I might as well let him answer his own question. "Who am I?" I watched him with curiosity.

"You have to remember, not ask somebody else," he said with a shrug of his small shoulders. "If you ask other people, all you end up with is their ideas about who they think you are and who they want you to be. What good is that?"

I took the bait, "I've always been independent!" I didn't like the idea of being a social construct. "I've worked on myself a lot. I can tell you who I am."

"O.K.. . . tell me," he replied, his face open and accepting.

"All right." I took a deep breath, "My name is Rick. I live in Boise, Idaho. I had a great childhood and usually, I'm a happy and optimistic person. I'm married with no children. I have a very nice home and a dog. I

11

have a master's degree in counseling. I'm a successful therapist who works primarily with survivors of abuse. I'm healthy and strong. Let's see, what else? I love to travel, I like to give workshops, I have good friends." I finished, feeling somewhat smug at the excellent presentation of my life and looked over at Daniel.

"Well, that's good!" He stopped for an instant and smiled gently at me. "That's all important stuff, but who acquired it?"

Acquired. The word stopped my mind. For one thing, it was an awfully big word for such a small person to use, but that wasn't really it. It was that particular word. To "acquire" means that you actually have to do something to get something. It's a word that describes action. His statement implied the existence of something which acted in order to be, or have, all of the things I had talked about. That was an odd thought.

I spoke slowly, "Daniel. . . are you saying that there's some part of me that I don't know about that decided to acquire all the stuff I just described? There's a part of me that all the rest of this just kind of belongs to?"

The little boy smile was back. "Yep. That's it. You just forget when you're on the Earth, then you have to remember who you are!"

I considered what he said and got ready to ask another question. With that, he disappeared, the windchime laugh fading quickly into complete silence.

Chapter 3

"Daniel, wait. . . wait! What do I do? Where do I go? I can't remember!"

Turning around, I could find no sign of the child. Suspended in the clouds, I was completely alone.

Think. Think. Think. The plane is gone, I'm out here with no one to help me. Where was that little boy? My mind pounded like forced labor in a quarry, working to convince me I was suffering from drug ingestion. He's not an hallucination, another part of me argued back. But what else could he be?

Whatever he is, I decided, I've got to find him. Without him, I'll never get back. Back to where? The plane, the ground, sanity? How could he leave me out here like this? What was I saying? How could I be out here? Something deep inside me began to suggest that while finding Daniel was urgent, it had to do with going forward and not back.

Think. Think. Think. What do you do when you're lost? Stop and think. O.K., think, think, think. I looked around as wispy snow white clouds went by me without concern. Where could he have gone?

"Daniel!" I yelled as loud as I could, only hoping for a response. Nothing. He was my escort through this strange experience; how would I survive without him? This wasn't the kind of thing you do by yourself.

I had seen so many clients who were afraid of flying. Some were worried about a crash, others obsessed about the fact only a piece of metal barred them from a deathly fall. But here I was, somehow suspended in the air. The clouds wandered around me, separating to accommodate my presence. I didn't seem to be going anywhere.

Perhaps I was not falling, but I had no idea where I was or how to get back on the plane. The little boy had told me nothing I could make any sense of. Turning around again, I saw nothing but more clouds. Profoundly alone, I had no answers to my dilemma.

"Come on, Daniel, tell me how to do this! Tell-me-what-to-do!" I shouted in frustration.

Silence. I had no idea how to get back on the plane I had left at 35,000 feet. Hysteria crept in and I began to laugh. Think. Think. What did he say? I didn't need to try to fly, I wasn't on drugs and. . . remember who you are. . . it's easy. What was he talking about?

Having no choice, I decided to try again to answer his question. I am. . . I am. . . I am what? I don't know, damn it! I need help here! Help from whom? The only one who could help me was me, I thought. But, I'm just a guy who was contentedly riding along when all of this started. Now, I'm out here without a plane! I should be falling and I'm not. Who is it that's not falling? It can't be me as I know me, that's impossible.

"Tell me!" I bellowed. "Tell me who I am!" Instantly, everything changed.

Replaced by a vast empty darkness, the clouds were gone. Glittering stars, far, far away made my loneliness seem infinite. I turned, faintly hoping to find Daniel behind me. My breathing stopped, paralyzed by the sight of the exquisite blue sphere, turning slowly in the silence. . . Earth.

Chapter 4

"Ladies and gentlemen, this is your captain speaking. Out the left side of the airplane you can see. . ." I peeled myself off the ceiling of the plane, heart pounding and adrenalin coursing through every cell of my body.

"Jesus!" I blurted. The man in the seat across the aisle was silent, but a smug appraisal of me occupied his eyes. He seemed to feel a perverse pleasure in watching another human being re-enter waking reality at super-sonic speed. Body trembling, I deliberately slowed my breathing and worked to gain control of my shattered feelings.

"Hi!" Happy eyes found mine and the little face broke into a big grin. He had his tray table down and several books with bright covers were stacked in front of him. "I really like this one a lot," he said enthusiastically. "It's a really, really good story. Want to read it?"

I stared at him, mouth slightly ajar, at once confused and extremely grateful to find myself back to normal. Back from where? What a terrible dream, an absolute nightmare. The little hand still held the favorite book out to me. I felt afraid to touch it, afraid to get lost again in the horrifying experiences. God, it had felt so real. I closed my eyes for a second, processing through the residual fear.

"Would you like something to drink, Sir?" I tracked the voice before cracking my eyes just wide enough to see a kind, smiling face inquiring from the aisleway.

"Something to drink, Sir?" she repeated.

"Uh, yeah. . . yeah that would be good." I needed something to soothe the nerves a little, quiet the mind.

"What would you like?" Her cheerfulness was reassuring. Whenever I had gotten nervous on an airplane, I always looked at the flight attendants to see if they were all right. If they continued to smile, I would relax.

Random thoughts ricocheted through my head. Everything had been so vivid only a moment ago, it seemed strange I should have to speak my words. Couldn't she just hear them? Didn't she know what I needed? But, this was the real world. People stand and stare mutely at you when you don't answer.

"I'll take a scotch and soda," I said perfunctorily.

The words sounded very strange coming out of my mouth. I had always felt people who knew immediately what they wanted to drink must drink frequently. If you hunted around and said something like, "Well, let's see, I'll have a. . . no. . . gee. . . what sounds good? I can never think of anything. . . oh maybe just a beer. . . no, how about. . . do you have any white wine. . . a small glass. . . ," all this meant that you seldom drank.

"That will be three dollars," she said as she lowered my tray table.

I handed her three one dollar bills and thought of my father. When I was little, he showed me how to fold a dollar bill back upon itself length-wise and make George Washington's endless forehead meet with the top of his high-necked white shirt so it looked like a giant toadstool. I had repeated this magical transformation with countless audiences and it was always a sort of private tribute to my father, even if it was at the expense of the father of our country. History never did command my respect.

Actually, it was history teachers who demolished my interest. I have heard tales of brilliant historians who made the events of centuries gone by come alive in the tombs of sophomore history classes. Somehow, they were able to convince the ghosts of generals, kings and statesmen alike to return from long-silent battlefields and drawing rooms and descend to give guest lectures for the spring semester. But, I had been sentenced to an endless procession of teachers who had become terminally bored. With skin pallid like the underside of a frog, and lonely monotone voices powered by asthmatic breath, they labored unsuccessfully to install the dates for all the events in human history permanently into my mind.

You learn a lot about time in school. Those round black-rimmed wall clocks with black numbers, black hands and a red sweep second hand marked off the minutes and hours of my formal education with excruciating accuracy. It wasn't that I hated school. Actually, I did very well, except for history. It's just that an adolescent experiences the most complex mixture of human emotional events imaginable. I am certain the gods created sophomore males on a celestially slow afternoon, solely for their own amusement. Take one body, sprinkle it with acne, remove all ability to speak coherently in the presence of cheerleaders and give it a recurring erection with no sense of social timing. . . cruel cosmic folly.

I sipped my drink and wondered how they made tubular ice cubes with holes in the middle and remembered the promises I had made to myself in the middle of the nightmare. I would check into that wonderful hotel and enjoy myself, forget the whole thing.

I love the endless stream of hot water provided by a hotel shower. Ever since I was a child, I would sometimes sit on the floor of the shower and let the water run over me. If you plug your ears, the sound of the water on your skull is greatly amplified. With eyes closed and lights off, I would imagine myself, huddled and soaked in a wonderful storm with magically warm rain.

In recent years, the activity has become a ritual that is almost sacred. When I allow myself this gift, I become like a small child again. Responsibilities and problems do not exist as the warm thundering of water caresses me and moves me beyond the limits of time and space to the greatest privacy that can be found. Pulling me from the heights of transcendent fantasy, my first wife would pour a glass of cold water over me if she discovered my ceremony. "Irreconcilable differences, Your Honor."

Finally, I turned back toward Daniel and took the book. Maybe it would help to read it. By the time we were finished, the food would be ready. A drink, food, read a story to the real little boy, make the feelings left over from that terrible dream go away.

Daniel looked at me with an expectancy found only in the eyes of a child. How simple he was. How complicated adult life was by comparison. I could make his whole day just by giving my attention and taking the time to read a story. I looked into the innocent, open face, utterly incapable of protecting himself from whatever I might put out. He was so totally present with me, his mind nowhere else but right on me.

I was the center of his world at this moment, the sun all the planets must ask for directions. And yet, he was far from empty. This little person was filled with intelligence and hope, courage and dedication to being alive.

What happens to us? How does all of that get replaced, bit by bit, cell by cell, with such heaviness? I couldn't imagine what could happen in my own life that would bring the level of happiness I saw in Daniel's face at the simple prospect of having a story read to him.

Where did it go, that part of me? I know how to enjoy myself as well as the next guy, but this was pure. It didn't have anything at all to do with impressing somebody or getting something. It had nothing to do with winning or protecting secrets or keeping an image up.

I remembered my attempts at conversation with other little kids. No wonder it had never worked. I was busy being numb while they were alive. I didn't really care about what school they went to and they knew that. I didn't care about making real contact with them and they knew that, too. The pity in their eyes, what else could be felt watching somebody work so hard to avoid being himself?

Be yourself, easy to say and hard to do. So many responsibilities, things to take care of; little things, big things, money, reputation, what does everyone think of me? Worse. Maybe they don't think of me! Reminds me of the famous line from Casablanca when Blackie says to Humphrey Bogart, "You hate me, don't you, Rick?" Bogey pauses a perfect particle of eternity and says, "I probably would if I gave you any thought." God, maybe they don't even notice you at all; the ultimate blow.

What changes along the way? Daniel wanted to be noticed, too, but not for an image he produced for me. All he wanted was some company in his own existence. He offered an invitation to join with him as he was, in the process of being even more of himself. Simple.

I thought about my "close" relationships. "Close" to me translated into time spent doing something with other people. I have "basketball friends." I have "go to lunch friends." I have "workout friends." We talk about what we've been doing, not how hard it can be sometimes to just keep going. We never mention how demoralizing it is when you realize you're so afraid to make someone unhappy, you have to come up with "what's right" and it might have nothing to do with what you want or who you really are. We don't talk about the incredible fear of "not making it," ending up with nothing and no one.

Even when I'm with my best friends, we sometimes play "pee on the wall." That's an old male game, who's got more, who's first, who's strongest, who's best. How can you ever talk about what's inside if the game is who's the biggest? Hell, I don't even know most of the time what's inside.

I used to know, just like Daniel does. I used to know what I wanted, what felt good and what didn't. I knew the people I wanted to be with and the ones that I didn't. There were no obligatory social requirements. I never even had to say "hi" to anyone, even if they said it to me. I remember when my days had to do with sitting in a tall tree watching the birds zoom in and out, when a burst of yellow butterflies was enough to send elation into my heart. I can remember being real. What happens to us?

There are so many rules and regulations about how we are supposed to behave. Things important and things mundane; they all come with specific instructions that cannot be broken. Riding on an elevator, for example. Nobody ever looks at anyone else when they are in an elevator. It would be a blatant violation of Code 3.2 Section 4 of the Otis Manual for Elevator Etiquette: "All persons occupying an elevator in the presence of one or more persons shall refrain from looking at one another during ascent, descent or button pressing. All persons riding an elevator in the presence of another person, known or unknown to the aforementioned occupant shall be required to watch the numbers over the door. . . and said occupants shall limit their conversation to one of the following phrases, any of which is to be spoken in a noticeably soft and non-intrusive tone: 1) Which floor? 2) Heading down (up)? 3) Go ahead. 4) Sorry (for use in situations where 6 or more persons are occupying said elevator.)" It goes on to suggest that such statements as "Are we moving?" "I got stuck in one of these for 2 hours once," and "I guess it doesn't matter if we exceed the weight limit as long as we're going down, right!" only tend to provoke panic and should be avoided at all costs.

"Are you going to read?" The small voice searched me out and I was glad to be found, no longer resentful about my company on the long flight. I had not read a child's book since I was little myself. There was a place in me that seemed happy about reading a story; a place I had forgotten all about.

I sighed deeply and answered, "Yes, I'd like to read the book, Daniel. It looks like a good one." Turning it over, I opened the bright cover. In big, bold orange letters, the title screamed up at me: Remember Who You Are.

Chapter 5

"Where did you get this?" My voice sounded sharper than I had meant it to, but I was scared. "Remember who you are." That's what Daniel had said to me in the dream, right before he left me alone out there.

Ignoring my question, the little boy said, "Here, turn the page. It's so cool."

Fingers pulling at the paper, he brought me face to face with an image that took my breath away. Heart tripping over itself, I stared down at the page. In front of me was the bright blue sphere, and it began slowly to turn.

"See!" His voice was excited, happy and far away. I looked up. Daniel stood twenty feet away from me. Twenty feet! Again, the plane was gone.

"Isn't this great?" His smile moved him closer to me. Beyond us, the Earth rotated in the darkness.

I managed to force words past the barricade of fear in my throat, "Oh God, Daniel. What is happening to me?"

"You're doing better," he answered brightly. "You remembered you didn't have to try to fly!" Peals of laughter filled the quiet.

"You looked so funny," he choked out. He was like any other little kid, face turning red, gasping for air, chest heaving, out of control over something he found desperately amusing.

Running out of patience I cried, "Do you think this is easy? Planes disappearing, finding out I can stand in space! One minute life is normal, the next it's crazy. I don't think this is funny at all."

Daniel stopped laughing and looked toward the Earth. "Isn't she beautiful?" he said, his voice filled with emotion. Then moving away from me, he announced, "Let's go. We have a lot to do."

He looked at me strangely, "You still don't remember?"

"Please don't start that again," I replied irritably. "I don't remember who I am. I can't. Just tell me and get it over with." I stared at him indignantly and asked, "Who am I, Daniel? And don't leave me out here again to figure it out."

I refused to blink, thinking perhaps if I looked at him hard enough, this would all make sense. At least, if I kept him in my sight, he wouldn't vanish. The blue eyes locked with mine. We stared at each other like Jeffrey Collins and I used to do in the fifth grade. Life depended on not blinking first. The one who lost would suffer at the judgment of the twenty-seven other kids who found this game so interesting. Clenched in ocular combat, the eyes would begin to burn and water. The classroom would blur and an overwhelming command to blink would finally be obeyed by the tortured lids and down they would fall, all honor and pride descending with them. I wasn't going to blink this time. I didn't dare. The idea that Daniel could disappear again was too frightening.

"O.K.," he said sweetly, blond lashes dipping past his eyes.

"O.K.?" I was surprised and pleased and totally unsure of what I had won.

"O.K. I'll tell you." He shrugged his shoulders and allowed his hands to fall together, looking like a miniature major league pitcher getting set to launch a fast ball.

"Really?" Relief flooded through me, "That's great. O.K., tell me."

"Actually, I have to show you," he replied with a smile. "That will work a lot better."

"O.K., fine. Show me." I had never liked relationship games which involved me trying to guess what someone else knows. I hated it when another person let me know he knew something and I'd be stuck trying to get it out of him. The variation of that game is starting to say something and trailing off with "never mind." That makes me crazy. I'll think about it constantly until I can get the rest of the information.

What did "remember who you are" mean? Was he talking about some reincarnation nonsense? That makes me crazy, too. Everybody used to use the "what's your sign" line. Now it's "I was Marie Antoinette, who were you?" Nobody was ever a potato farmer who lived a normal life with a nice wife and six kids. These people are always an emperor or part of a harem or Christopher Columbus. In a few years, everyone will have been Elvis or Marilyn Monroe.

Meanwhile, I'm standing out in space, talking to a seven year-old about things I don't understand and feeling annoyed! What an odd transition I had made. Rushing past the utter panic, I was now impatient. I thought about how human beings do that. Something is only absolutely amazing for a very short time, then we move into tearing it apart. While consistently calling for the out of the ordinary experience, once we have it we attack with every discounting, cynical, intellectualizing ordinant we have. Then, we're disappointed and start the search again.

A Native American friend of mine told me one of the reasons the general population doesn't have visions is that we insist they can't exist. While we guard our cherished ideas so well that nothing can disturb them, we forget that a vision couldn't break into such a mental prison even if it did exist. Then we have our evidence. Visions do not exist because I do not have them. I do not have them because I believe they do not exist.

I really don't know. I've never had one. I've tried. Following the careful advice of a good teacher, I even went out to a supposedly magical place in the desert once and spent a whole day waiting for my vision. Nothing happened. But then, my mind stood in red alert the whole time, judging, labeling, watching, afraid at once I would see something and would not see something. I'm convinced if I had seen something, that same mind would have found a quick method for explaining it away. Anyway, that was the last of my attempts at visions. Until today.

Is that what this whole thing was? Some kind of vision about my life, one of those life-changing, "Given-By-God" things? Wasn't that supposed to include a great chorus of angels, the skies parting, a deep, resonant voice? If God was trying to tell me something, surely it wouldn't be through a little boy. If God wants you to hear a special message, isn't it more formal than this? Wouldn't it come at church or in a prayer or something?

People spend lifetimes in churches listening to well-trained ministers, burning candles, singing, offering communal prayers. That would seem to be the logical place for receiving edicts from God, not out here with a giggling, illogical child.

However, I never heard anything directly from God in church either. Obviously, most people hadn't. That kind of thing would get around very quickly and numbers would be going up, not down. Somehow, the idea that God would speak to a random congregation on a Sunday morning seemed highly unlikely. Of course, there were always reports of a statue crying somewhere in another country. I never knew what to do with that. If God wanted to say something, why bother with forcing tears out of marble? Wouldn't he just say it?

I grew up in a regular Methodist Church without crying statues or parting skies. I went to Sunday school where, under the watchful eyes of a blond, blue-eyed Jesus, we heard stories from the Bible, drew pictures and sang songs. Once a month, we joined with the whole congregation in the sanctuary for regular services. I found solace in the little pencils and pieces of paper mounted in special holders on the back of the pew in front of me. I would write messages to my friends, draw, make airplanes, anything to get through the endless combinations of words coming from the minister.

He stood up high, in a special kind of box. Dressed in a billowy, white robe, he would talk of things I could not understand. He sure looked important. I knew that he had some kind of special relationship with God, but I didn't know what it was. Behind him was an enormous stained-glass window depicting Jesus with a bunch of little children and some sheep. I had heard over and over that Jesus loved the little children, and I really liked the sheep, so that was O.K. But the minister sounded mad a lot of the time. Really mad.

He would boom out instructions to love Jesus, but I didn't understand how to love somebody I'd never even met. He talked about how much Jesus loved us and so we should love him back. This was really confusing. The minister was angry because I couldn't love a person I didn't know who already loved me for some mysterious reason.

And then, after all the words about love, suddenly this stirred-up authority would command us to, "Eat the body and drink the blood of Christ." I didn't even want to eat the sheep, let alone this person who supposedly loved me.

I grew to hate those excursions to the sanctuary. I tried to ask about this strange exercise everyone was so willing to perform. I was told, "We do this because we love Jesus." Back to that again.

As I got older and could grasp the idea of symbolism, of course the horror went out of this communal practice. But I still didn't understand it very well. When I asked for assistance, what came back was an explanation that didn't make sense to me, or more often, a crisp admonition that I didn't yet have a close enough relationship with Jesus to understand him. If I would only love him more, I would understand everything. There we were again.

. How do I love someone I can't understand and whom I've never met? "Pray," someone suggested.

Prayer, it always seemed like a strange idea to me. After all, what people asked for was sometimes ridiculous. They would try to gain God's attention so he would bestow good favor on them and they could win a baseball game or get a new house. I had known people who prayed to God for everything, like placing an order at McDonald's, pick it up at the second window. God couldn't really be some kind of clerk, taking requests and filling them at random. Everybody who went off to war prayed for safety and victory. Didn't the God of the other guys listen to them? What about when it was supposed to be the very same God, Christians against Christians or Moslems against Moslems?

Prayer. That's one of those things you're supposed to know how to do. Everyone around you seems to have it down. When someone makes that suggestion to another person, the only appropriate response is a knowing, calm, "Of course." This person then nods and looks knowingly at you. The message is, "we can do this expertly, as all good people should."

Of course, I know how to look appropriately serious. I know how to bow my head, although what to do with the hands seems open for debate. Once, I went to a Catholic Church with a friend. That was intimidating — all the kneeling and half-kneeling and sort of kneeling and getting prepared to kneel. Anyway, I would close my eyes and talk to God inside my head and say, "Amen" and get up with roughly the same effect as watering my house plants. It was a "should" without a pay-off, so it didn't last long. Certainly God never spoke to me and I never did meet Jesus.

Well into adolescence, I decided to accept the judgment of my irritated minister. According to him, I simply didn't appreciate the love Jesus offered and so, I was doomed. But, doomed to what? The Methodist Church was never clear about that, although they did say there was no hell with a devil in residence. I did learn God was out there somewhere, and he was undoubtedly very angry with me. Was it now time for me to meet God and get my well-deserved punishment?

"Well, are you coming?" Daniel's voice felt like an electrical shock.

"Coming where?" I stammered, more than half-convinced I was about to meet my Maker. After all, God was the only one who could be behind such a bizarre situation.

"Coming with me so I can show you who you are," he said, words full of the impatience any child directs toward an adult who has forgotten something perfectly obvious.

"Daniel. . ." I was afraid to form the rest of my question. "Are we going to see God?"

Exploding with laughter, he finally managed to wheeze out, "Of course not!"

"What is so funny?" I demanded, feeling insulted by his apparent insensitivity.

Past the spasms of merriment, I heard him say, "Why would anyone have to go see God?"

Chapter 6

After forty years of what my Sunday school teacher would describe as "Rebellion against God," I was finally admitting I would need to face Him. For decades, I had honed and polished my capacity to avoid the inevitable. Now, I was ready and this child found it hysterical.

Actually, I was far from ready. Who is ready? If you told the average person he would meet God in an hour, nobody would be ready. Everyone has some idea, even if it's vague, about what God expects. And we all know we haven't come anywhere near that. So, we put it off. We will think about it later, much later, when we're old, even better, when we're dying. It's definitely one of those "some day" propositions.

Even if you go to church every Sunday, you still screw it up. Going to church just reminds you of it more often. Not that I'm a terrible person. I've always thought I was a good person, but not good enough to meet God.

Meet God. . . oh my God. . . what would it mean? This is the day I will have to look at my whole life in excruciating detail and explain, one by one, my failings. Why didn't I do a better job? Why didn't I get any warning it was going to be today of all days? A man should have a chance to prepare for an audience with God. I'm not even dressed appropriately.

"Goddamn it!" I gulped hard, and wondered if all of those verbal indiscretions would be forgiven. The Ten Commandments. . . I couldn't remember what they were, but I was fairly sure I had done pretty well with those. I never killed anyone. I had never stolen anything. My mother and father were happy with the way I had treated them. That was three, what about the other seven?

Maybe God really would be like all those paintings from the Renaissance, big, bearded, angry, powerful. I was starting to panic. What would happen to me when God really took a good look at my life.

Suddenly, I remembered a major transgression committed when I was about ten. My parents had denied my demand for something I was sure was essential to my continued existence. Furiously angry, four words had flown out of my mouth, "I even hate God!"

The words went heavenward and, sailing out across Waverly Drive, they just cleared the Eason's house and went straight into God's ear. Terrified, I braced for the expected lightening bolt and tried to console myself. Surely, in all his wisdom, God would realize I really didn't mean it. The frustrated rantings of a child would not be taken as a serious statement of spiritual standing. The event was probably not really even recorded. Or if it was, definitely an asterisk would be warranted.

Why then, did I even remember it? Was it just something that that wound its way up to consciousness, having escaped from some aberrant brain cell? Could it be the first in a series of holographic incidents called up for review by God himself?

Maybe there really was a hell. The proselytizers who had rung my doorbell at profoundly inconvenient times on equally inconvenient days were sure of it. If we didn't do precisely the right thing, we would be condemned to a terrible eternity.

A friend told me a story she knew about an Episcopalian Bishop. On his way to the Cathedral one morning, dressed in full regalia, cope, miter and staff, he opened his front door to find these people. They took a look and a deep breath and then asked if they could come in and speak to him about his salvation! Always debonair, he had replied, "No thank you. But you may come with me so that I may speak to you about yours."

I actually invited them in once. After thirty minutes about the sins of mankind and the inevitable punishment coming from God, I had lost my patience and asked them to leave.

They did, having dumped a load of unwelcome pamphlets on my coffee table. Maybe I should have read their material. I had filed it in my trash can, having explained them away as crackpots, extremists, off the wall. Like the guy around town who rides a bike with a big sign on the back that says, "The Kingdom Of God Is At Hand. Repent." I had always wondered how on earth someone would conclude that he needed to do something like that.

Daniel stood by my sleeve. "It's all right," he said softly. His face was calm and gentle. He was no longer laughing, but amusement still played in his eyes. "Everything is perfectly all right."

"Daniel, please tell me what is going on." I was desperate for some answers and weary of the indecipherable puzzle. "I don't understand. I don't know where to go or what I'm supposed to do. Please tell me."

"Come with me," he replied quietly. "Come on. . . I'll show you."

Too tired to question him, I simply decided I would no longer fight. I would go with him and meet God. And with my decision, everything was forever changed.

Chapter 7

"What. . . what are we doing here?" Hardly able to believe my eyes, I exclaimed, "Daniel, what the hell are we doing in Boise, Idaho?"

I had grown up in this small city placed in the empty expanse of desert falling out from the Rocky Mountains. People used to make jokes about Boise, Idaho, but I liked living here. Beautiful wilderness rose up out of the barren sweep of sagebrush territory. Within minutes, you could find high mountains, big trees and white water.

Boise tended to be a good mile behind the trends generated from more sophisticated areas of the country. Like a rock dropped into calm water, changes from the big cities would ripple towards me and I could see them approaching from a long distance. That made it comfortable. I always had a chance to get prepared, decide what I wanted to do before anything ever reached me.

Out of the corner of my eye, I saw Daniel walking away. "Wait. Wait!" I called.

Thankful to find that my legs worked just fine now that they were back on terra firma, I caught up with him. We were in a park; the same park in which I had played softball, languished by the duck pond and flown my kite. It was a great park, but. . . "Daniel, I thought we were going to see God. What are we doing here? I thought we were going to see God. God's up, not down."

Daniel walked even faster, determination showing in his small, square jaw. I tried to get his attention, "How did we get here? Last thing I remember, we were in space. That's a long way. How did we get here so fast? Where are we going?"

He seemed obsessed with traveling as fast as he could and did not answer me. I couldn't imagine where he was going. What could be so important around here?

We were approaching the little kids' play area. I could see a tiny girl with a spectacular smile matching her new red sneakers. Mom at one end and dad at the other, she was working up the courage to go down the slide. In this moment, her entire world was made up of that shiny, silver slide and two people who obviously adored her.

Just like these kids, I used to ride the merry-go-round, swing high in the air, and race down the slide. It seemed like such an impossibly long time ago. Did Daniel want to go and play on the swings? Had we gotten off an airplane and come down from outer space so Daniel could ride on a swing?

I made another attempt to get an answer, "Daniel. . . Daniel. . . what are you doing? What's going on?" His hightops bit into the grass and he steadfastly headed for the playground equipment.

"Come on!" he said enthusiastically. Good. He had finally found his voice. "Let's play," he added.

I was amazed he could say such a thing, "Daniel, we can't play now! We're on our way to see God." But on he went, sloshing now through the sand and climbing up on the monkey bars.

"See, this is fun! Come and play," he laughed.

"Daniel, this is serious." Frustration filled my words, "We have to do something really important. We don't have time to play."

"There's always time to play," he replied, pulling himself up higher.

"No, there is not always time to play," I said with the moral imperative of a grownup who thinks he knows everything, " You play after you do the things that are important."

He tipped himself over backwards and hung upside down, an enormous smile filling his face, "See, there's always time to play, because play is important."

I wasn't sure whether that smile reflected pure pleasure at playing on the metal bars, or was the result of having gotten the best of me. Crouching down, I turned my head at an awkward angle, looked straight into his face and spoke slowly, "We don't have time for this."

"You just said we have to do the things that are important," he chirped. Now I was sure he was just out to drive me crazy.

Using that unique tone of voice usually restricted to third grade teachers who are about to lose their mind I said, "Daniel, get off the monkey bars and get back to work."

His smile only got bigger as he answered with, "Rick, get on the monkey bars and start to play. Just for a while. Come on. . . it's fun."

Clearly, my choices were to get terribly angry and hope he would choose to comply and do things my way, or I could give up. I decided to let the mockery of my discomfort pass by. After all, it seemed impossible to get him to go in any direction that I determined was right. Releasing my aggravation with a deep sigh, I grasped the bars and pulled myself up on top of the contraption and came to a sudden stop.

I remembered this. . . feeling ten feet tall, up above everyone else, able to see farther, looking down on the tops of the other kids' heads. I remembered the intense blue sky of summer overhead and the geese flying by. Hooking my legs around the bars, I allowed myself to fall backwards. My body turned upside down and I was surprised to hear a laugh fall out. For a few happy moments, I swung back and forth, watching the other kids play.

The "other kids." Listen to me. One minute on the monkeybars and I forget I'm a grownup. The rest of the adults must think I'm really strange. . . maybe one of those perverts that hangs around little kids in the park. I'd better get off before somebody complains.

"You have a right to play, too." Daniel's face grew closer and farther, closer and farther away as I swung back and forth. He was standing in the sand, looking concerned. I untangled my feet, flipped over and stood next to him. His ability to know what I was thinking was unnerving.

"How do you do that?" I asked him intently. "How do you know what's going on in my mind?"

"Let's go swing." The king of the nonsequiter settled himself into a swing, pumped his legs and set a course for the sky.

"O.K., O.K." I muttered. Somehow, I was not really displeased. After all, what could the harm be in taking some time to play in the park? I laughed out loud as I, too, flew high in the air. Why not? After what I had been through today, why not?

Chapter 8

I looked out across fields of green surrounding the swings as I used my legs to push me higher. Daniel was right beside me, wearing a grin almost too big for his face.

"See, this is really fun!" he called out, his body passing by on its way backwards as I went forward. I had to admit, it was fun. Actually, it was great!

I thought about how long it had been since I had been on the swings. . . probably adolescence. I think I took a girl to the park after a dance one night. It was one of those romantic things you try to come up with to impress your date. On that lovely moonlit night, pushing her on the swings, hearing her laugh, knowing she was happy, I was busy calculating the next move. I guess that really didn't count as my last time on the swings.

In my final spring at grade school, I went out to the playground late one afternoon and sat on the swings for a little while. I was feeling strangely sad. For an entire year, I had looked forward to escaping elementary school and joining with the big kids. Suddenly, the time to leave was here and all I could feel was an empty, hollow place inside my chest. This aching spot grew at an incredible pace until it threatened to swallow me up, leaving nothing behind but my tears.

I sobbed that day, hands clenched around the metal links holding up the swing. I cried for everything I was leaving behind. Somehow, what was coming didn't make up for what was to be lost. Memories from my little-boy collection came up, one after the other, each setting off a new round of grief.

I thought about the way the old school smelled of books and crayons and peanut butter sandwiches. The yellow lights high up above would shine down on the brown linoleum floors that Mr. Brewer polished a hundred times a week. I thought about my teachers, even the ones I hadn't liked that much. And the playground, all the games I won and lost on the bumpy expanse of green grass, the sound of the sprinkler system at the end of the day and running as fast as I could to get to the basketball hoops first. It was so important to set up a stake so my friends and I could fly high and dribble low.

When this summer came to an end, I would not be entering through the same glass doors, looking for my name on the assignment sheet tacked up in the principal's office and finding my way to a new classroom. This building would no longer be the comfortable place I had come to rely on. I would no longer see the faces I had depended on to keep me safe. Furthermore, I would not be allowed to be the same person I had been.

I was not going to be able to cry like this, I decided. I couldn't go on baby equipment, like swings. Somehow, I would have to know everything, and not ask stupid questions. If I got scared, I would have to pretend I was strong.

I thought about it all and grudgingly left it behind in one intense, private ceremony of loss. Once I heard somebody say that everything in life is a trade-off. That day I traded my childhood for my adolescence and once done, it seemed gone forever. Lost in my thoughts, I had not noticed that Daniel had stopped swinging. He sat motionless, his feet planted in the sand.

"What's the matter?" I tossed out my inquiry, hoping the reply would allow me to continue to play.

"Look," he said so quietly, I was not certain I had heard him correctly. I slowed down and asked him again, only to hear the same one word answer.

"Look at what? I don't see anything," I stated. Now at a full stop, my gaze was fixed in the same direction as his, but I could not find anything unusual. Glancing over at him, I found he had started across the park. Even as I was running after this mysterious child, I considered how important he had become in such a short time. After all, nothing had been the same since I first saw him.

The last thing I could consider "normal" was sitting on a plane on my way to London. Since then, I had been out to space and down to Boise and away to see God. Anyway, that's where I thought we were going. When I took a moment to think about it, I realized Daniel had never said we were going to see God.

"Daniel. . . hey, Daniel." I tried to talk to him as we hurried along but he was quiet as we steadily approached the far side of the park. "Are we going to see God? Is that what this whole weird thing is all about? Can't you just stop and tell me what is going on?"

With a resolve impossible to alter, the boy continued on his course and I decided I might as well go along with him. After all, protesting never even got his attention.

We walked together for what seemed like an hour. I had been down these roads so many times before. Funny how things look different when you're a kid. Every street held an adventure, especially if you were accompanied by at least one other kid.

That house on the corner had the best tree on the whole block. If you could climb up fast enough without provoking some adult's announcement that it was too dangerous, you could see forever. And, if you were up first, you got to decide who else could come up. What a powerful feeling that was, like owning the whole world.

Over there, right behind that garage was a steep, weedy hill, the ultimate challenge to childhood courage. We would gather up a big piece of cardboard, sit on it and shove off. Out of control, the paper sled would careen down the hill, bucking screaming children from its back like some primitive beast. Great glory came to anyone who could stay onboard.

Daniel and I continued to walk silently, crossing over the river which chased itself all the way through the city. I had spent wonderful hours sloshing along in that water, catching pollywogs and setting them free again. The slick, deep green mud at the bottom would squish between my toes and my mind would create wild stories of adventure and heroism. I was so alive.

I guess those precious gifts of childhood were simply the result of freedom from responsibility. A child has time to do whatever he wants to do. He has no worries; the adults do everything for him. Once childhood is gone, it's gone. You have work and responsibilities and the next generation gets to play. That's the way it is supposed to be.

Walking under the graceful arms of the oak trees along the street, I felt a sensation in my chest. A deep sadness pushed up and challenged the conventional logic which had seemed to make perfect sense a moment ago. Even as a small trickle of water can make its way through seemingly impenetrable cement, I found myself feeling something I hadn't allowed for a long time. Suddenly all of that logic was only a comfortable explanation for what really was a tragic loss.

A child's exquisite ability to be alive, to be in rhythm with himself, was not due to having more time. He just hadn't closed himself off and shut down his capacity to respond to the gifts of the moment. He was still able to see everything and feel everything. He wasn't carrying around a list of instructions about how to control it all.

I used to be like that! Bit by bit, my openness and connection with everything that is, got replaced by heaviness and fear. The man became a container for concerns about an artificial life. Who thinks what of me? What will I do if this happens? How am I going to pay my bills? How can I get what I want? The child that knew how to be alive, where did he go? Had I managed to kill him off?

It's not time that goes away, it's our very essence that gets destroyed. Focused on what we have to do, we never even notice the absence of that purest part of ourselves. And without it, life becomes only an obstacle course, an endless series of problems to be solved.

I looked carefully at the boy beside me. He stopped, turned and smiled before saying softly, "That's it, Rick. That's it."

Chapter 9

No longer surprised at his ability to read my mind, I accepted the slip of his hand into mine and responded with the passion I was feeling, "Daniel... what happens to us? I want to be the way I used to be. I want to feel the way I used to feel."

"You just get mixed up," he replied. "Every time you come here, it takes a long time just to figure out that you're all mixed up. Then, you get started figuring it out, and you usually don't have enough time left over to do that, so you just have to try to remember all over again. I don't know why it works like that, but it does."

He conveyed this strange assortment of information in a completely matter of fact way. In fact, he seemed oddly cheerful about it. I felt like I had just listened to a child's review of a movie. It almost makes sense, but you really can't put the pieces together.

Confusion crossed my face and I said, "I'm afraid I don't understand."

"Of course you don't understand!" he said emphatically. "How can you understand something if you can't remember? That's why it's so hard. You have to know to look for something even though you don't remember it at all."

I tried unsuccessfully to make sense of his words. "Daniel, I don't have any idea what you're talking about." I did not feel impatient with him, only anxious to have information that was clearly going to be very important to me. "Can you back up and explain what you're saying?"

He took in an enormous breath and started again, "You don't remember that you don't remember until you know you have something you have to remember. Then, you start to remember and it gets better, but usually not better enough before you forget again."

36

He smiled, pleased at his apparent accomplishment. I was stopped. Clearly, he was trying to tell me something I needed to know, but the harder he tried, the more it sounded like gibberish to me. I did my best to glean something out of his sentences.

I ventured a simple guess, "I need to remember something?"

"How do you know that you know something?" he replied with a challenge.

That was a question I had an answer for, "Well, it comes easily to mind. You don't have to struggle with it. You're confident about it."

He looked at me for a moment and then asked, "Suppose something was true in your head, but wasn't true anywhere else. . . how would you know?"

"Evidence." That was easy. Everyone knew that empirical evidence was the hallmark of truth. I looked over at him with a new sense of assurance.

He was not satisfied with my simple answer. "Suppose what you call 'evidence' was only what you saw because it was the only thing you knew to look for and there was a lot of other stuff you never even noticed?" I had seen the same odd expression on his face right before he disappeared and left me to figure things out for myself.

I said softly, "Well, I guess you'd end up with only part of the truth. . . the part you knew to look for." Daniel's eyes met mine and I suddenly felt like Christopher Columbus was about to tell me the world wasn't flat any more.

"Right!" he said enthusiastically. "What if the stuff you didn't even know to look for was way bigger than the stuff you knew?" He smiled up at me, an action I was beginning to regard with a peculiar anxiety.

"It would have to catch up with you eventually. . ." I trailed off as my stomach sent up a warning the world was about to shift sideways.

"Yep. . . well, it's caught up," he said, walking off in a new direction. "Come on, there's something I want you to see."

"Wait a minute. Wait!" I stumbled after him, "I don't want any more confusion than I already have. Daniel, I don't want to see anything. Unless, are we going to meet God now? Are you finally going to take me there?"

Starting mid topic, he replied, "I always thought it would be a good idea to just show somebody what it's all about. They just keep sending teacher after teacher to Earth and what happens? Usually, the people find a way to get rid of the teacher. Look what happened to Jesus!"

He stopped speaking and I struggled to find a way to understand what he had just said. "Daniel, are you talking about God. . . the angels. . . is God about to reveal himself ?"

There it was once again, the rippling, cascading laughter. His amusement about my questions was really getting to be insulting. I was doing the best I could do. My God. . . what a day! How did he expect me to respond? But I did have to admit, whenever he giggled everything somehow seemed manageable again.

The little boy threw up his arms and said, "Rick, you just have to know about God, don't you?" He watched my confusion for a second and continued, "See, that's what keeps getting all the people in such trouble. . . they have to know about God and so, they keep making things up to explain what they don't really know. I told everybody, we should just let one person see everything, then it wouldn't be so hard to get their attention."

"See everything?" I sputtered, afraid of what might happen next.

His voice sounded a little chagrined, "Well, everybody's so lost, you can't find anything, especially yourselves! When somebody tries to help you, you never listen."

Completely confused, I said, "I don't understand what you are talking about. I'm sorry."

I knew it was important. I knew I should understand. But, I was lost in a familiar sense of muddled confusion. A very specific feeling always came up in me when anything supremely important was going on. With a complete certainty that it was essential to take something in, my mind would flood with importance and come to a terrible halt.

Not hesitating long enough to allow me to catch up, Daniel continued to talk. "See, I think every time a teacher is sent, all he can do is talk a lot. When he talks a lot, the people hear what they have already learned and they never understand what he says. They get so happy when they can take something really big and get it all squished down into something really little. But once it's squashed, it's squashed, know what I mean?"

He looked up at me with his bright, open face and I dared to give answering his question my best shot. "Daniel, are you saying somebody out there keeps sending teachers to the Earth so that people can understand God, but nobody ever comprehends what they say?"

He looked as though he would like to affirm my effort and then replied, "Sort of. . . kind of. . . well, that's not exactly right. . . but. . ."

I took in another deep breath. "Tell me again."

Copying me, he drew in an enormous breath and said, "Well, it's more like the truth keeps showing up, but nobody wants to listen."

I remained confused, "Isn't that the same thing?"

"Sort of. . . kind of," he started.

I finished the familiar sentence for him, "Well, that's not exactly right. . ."

His eyes searched mine for understanding as he said, "See, people always want to know what reality is. What's the truth? What they never get is that there are bunches of truths and realities all at the same time. We try to tell them that, but they never like it! They always say, 'Yes, but what is really true?' It depends on how you know how to look and what kind of a heart you have."

"That's not so hard to understand, Daniel," I said with relief. "Everybody knows that people see things differently."

He quickly removed any sense of comfort I might have created. "They might know about people's different opinions about stuff, but they sure don't know about how people live in different worlds."

My heart sank, "What?"

His attitude was matter of fact. "People. . . they live in different worlds. . . you know, depending on what kind of heart and way of seeing they have. A really long time ago, people could see and know everything, but they forgot. Want to know why?"

With more irritation than I intended, I cried, "Of course I want to know why. Daniel, I haven't come all this way to bail out now! What happened? Why did they forget?"

Four simple words changed everything. "See how it is!"

Chapter 10

I was getting used to this business of instantly being somewhere else. It had possibilities; maybe I could learn to think myself over to London, instead of enduring the usual eleven hour flight. Perhaps I could learn how to get myself to the office without a car.

"Where are we?" I asked quietly, looking out over a lovely, green valley.

He smiled, "We're not in Boise, any more. But it really doesn't matter where we are. People do the same thing all over the Earth. They think they are different from each other. . . you know, those lines they draw on the maps. . . they treat them like they're real. What a silly idea to think you can divide the Earth up and pretend everybody's different, by sitting somewhere and drawing lines on a piece of paper. . . don't you think that's a funny thing to do?"

His eyes locked with mine and I didn't know what to say. It had never really occurred to me that it truly was a ridiculous concept. I remembered reading somewhere, I think it was Chief Joseph of the Nez Perce people who said, "We are all alike, brothers of the one father and one mother, with one sky above us and one government for all. When we live this, then the great spirit chief who rules above will smile upon this land and send rain to wash out the bloody spots from the face of the Earth that were made by brothers' hands."

I felt ashamed of myself. I had seen those beautiful words and had put them aside as "romantic Indian lore." I know there are many wonderful pieces of wisdom from the first people on the continent of America, but I had placed the ideas in the "irrelevant column," leftovers from history. The same place I put anything that has to do with the "universal brotherhood of man" theme. . . a glorious idea that never works. Most of us can't even get along with our auto mechanic, let alone somebody from the other side of the world.

We all get misty eyed around Christmas time, but the feeling vaporizes as quickly as the illusion that we really had enough money to pay for all the things we were seduced into buying. January depression. . . bills and that sinking realization that worldwide peace and harmony is a great dream; too bad it doesn't work out that way. What was this child trying to tell me?

"So, what happened, Daniel? You started to tell me about how people used to be able to see everything and know everything. I just want to say, that's very contrary to what we're taught. I mean, humans rose up out of the animals and we are getting better and better at managing ourselves and the world. We're more intelligent, not less."

"Is it intelligent to murder yourselves and destroy your home?" he asked softly. I was surprised to see his blue eyes fill with tears. "While you are busy counting how many more machines you can build, your people are suffering all over the planet. Do you want to know why?"

"Yes, yes, tell me why." Did he really have an answer to such an enormous question?

He took in another deep breath and answered, "Well, you guys live in the mud and you make more of it every day. That's what's really sad. I think that if we could just get you to stop doing that kind of stuff, everything would. . . "

"Wait, wait. . . hold it!" The engine was rolling down the tracks without the rest of the train. What the hell was he talking about? I found myself cracking my knuckles one at a time, a peculiar trait which reveals itself only when I am under stress. Flying all over the place without a coherent companion qualifies as stress. . . extreme stress.

Calmly watching my socially unacceptable behavior, Daniel suddenly blurted out, "Whoops, I forgot."

I balefully stared at him and continued to abuse my fingers.

He shrugged his small shoulders and said, "I forgot, you don't remember about density."

I found my voice, "Density. . . that word means something thick to me."

"That's a good way to understand it," he replied brightly. "See, everything is made up of energy and it's all moving really quick. . . you know that from school, right?"

"Well, that's elementary physics, yes," I answered, feeling quite intelligent.

He was filled with enthusiasm, "O.K. . . if something moves really fast without being blocked and its atoms are really far apart, then what?"

"Well, it's lighter, more transparent, less. . . less in the way." Good, I liked having the answers to his questions for a change.

His little face looked at me with an odd intensity, "Rick, do you mean you could see through it more easily. . . see what might be beyond it?"

"I suppose so. That would be one of the characteristics," I affirmed.

He nodded, apparently happy I could follow what he was saying. "So, what was meant to be light and translucent got all messed up and slowed down and got very thick and ran into itself and everything else. . . like when the power goes off. . . makes that sound. . . RRRrrrUUmmmmm. . . you know, slow. That's what I meant when I said you were all living in the mud."

I felt I had suddenly taken a wrong turn and was about ready to fall off the trail. "Are you telling me that the energy of Earth itself used to be different?"

He gazed up for a second and said, "Kind of. . . sort of. . ."

I knew my part, "Not exactly."

"See, Earth's energy itself would be fine if all the people who lived on the Earth didn't build up density." His eyes took in the natural scene around us, "It's not Earth that's the problem. . . it's the choices people keep making."

"I don't understand," I replied, uncertain I really wanted to risk asking for clarification.

But he was ferociously intent on increasing my understanding and quickly went on, "Before you built up density, your energy was moving really fast, and the Earth's energy was moving really fast, too. You were able to work together. But, by making the choices you make over and over again, it all gets filled up and thick and heavy and you lose all of your abilities. Next thing you know, the only thing you consider is the stuff you can find with your body senses. . . you know, what you can see and taste and smell and hear. . . just the obvious. Then you have to do everything at a thick level and you just get more and more angry and upset and hurt each other and the Earth."

I was still confused. "I guess I don't understand what density has to do with how we treat each other."

He thought for a moment and continued, "Well, when everything slows way down, that makes it look like there's such a thing as something solid. If something's solid, then it's separate from the next thing that's solid. People start to see things in a really limited way. I mean, if everything's solid and separate, then you have to make sure you compete with the other people to get what you need. . . because, if it's all unconnected, you can't just receive what you need.

"People start to fight for survival with their hands and weapons. Things have to be either won or lost. Stuff you need has to be pulled out of the Earth with a lot of pain. Other people turn into objects. . . things to be moved around and used by one another. It's really awfully sad. . . " he said, walking off through some wildflowers.

Following behind him, I found myself wanting to argue, but curiously, I didn't have much enthusiasm for it. "Daniel, competition is necessary. . . that's how we get what we need. . . " I trailed off, unable to continue with something that was clearly not correct. "Tell me another way. . . "

His little face lit up at my willingness to learn, "Well, somebody who is full of density can only make something that matches that. If he can only use his senses because all the rest of his abilities are clogged up, he struggles really hard and ends up with only what he can make out of the most obvious stuff. Maybe that wouldn't be so sad except that he doesn't even know he's doing that! He thinks reality exists outside of himself and that he's just supposed to recognize it. But really, he creates his own world. He can use density to create with or he can do it with truth.

"See, there's so much more that you could use when you make your reality. Instead people limit themselves and make systems to decide what things can be real and what can't. But, they're only using what they know to include and exclude, not really determining what's imaginary and what's true. Excluding something only makes it non-existent for the person that did the excluding. It doesn't really affect its existence in reality.

"Isn't this the most beautiful thing?" He had stopped and crouched down over a tiny green thing. I peered over his shoulder.

"What is it?" My voice conveyed a desire to be polite.

"See, Rick," he said sadly. "That's what I mean. Your mind immediately wants to put a name on it, take it apart, put it in its place as something dangerous or something safe to ignore. But look at it closely."

I had gotten somewhat used to the fact that I was going to have to do things that did not make sense to me if I was going to continue being in the company of this little guy. I knelt down beside him and gingerly reached out my finger to touch the little plant.

"What do you see?" he asked quietly.

I didn't know what he wanted me to say, "I see some sort of plant my wife would know all about. She can grow anything. The garden at home is full of all kinds of different. . ."

He interrupted my rambling speech. "You see, your mind wants to pull you far away from where you really are. Don't let that happen, Rick. What do you see?"

I stared uncomfortably at the little growing thing. It appeared to be some kind of fern. . . no, he said not to name it. "Well, it's a bright green plant of some sort." There. I hoped I had done something right.

"What else?" He stared at me and waited with a patience I wished he would run out of.

I gave it another try, "It seems to be doing quite well. . . I mean, it doesn't look brown or anything." What did he want from me?

"What else? What else can you see, Rick?" The voice was very, very faint and the world had gone completely green.

Chapter 11

Jumping to my feet, I expected to pull clear of the all encompassing color. Instead, I found myself surrounded by spectacular beauty. Enormous, vibrant trees swayed around me, like giant drifts of seaweed caught on a gentle current. Emerald green, they were unlike anything I had ever seen before.

"Daniel," I whispered as I slowly turned around. "Where am I?"

The little voice seemed to bypass my ears; I simply heard him clearly in my mind. "What do you see? Tell me what you see, Rick."

For the moment unconcerned the boy did not seem anywhere nearby, I answered quietly, "I'm in some kind of forest. Daniel, there are the most incredibly beautiful trees here!"

I heard him repeat, "Tell me what you see."

My heart was full of appreciation at the vision before me. Not wanting to miss any of it, I almost forgot to answer him. "They're moving somehow, opening and closing what appear to be giant fans. I didn't know trees like this existed. Daniel, are we in the Rain Forest?"

"What do you see?" he repeated wordlessly.

I allowed my feet to take a few steps forward and took in a wider view before I responded, "Astounding beauty! These trees, they are as graceful as ballet dancers, moving back and forth together as if music must be playing somewhere." I paused to watch them and suddenly realized what they were doing, "They're reaching for the sunshine! Daniel, they're stretching upwards, spreading out their leaves like glorious, translucent fans."

I knew he wanted me to continue. "I can see the sun coming down inside them! The trees. . . now they have become transparent somehow. I can see the sun moving down through them in sparkling bits of light. It's just pouring into them and flowing freely around once inside. God, it's breathtaking; everything is moving, the light, the trees and it smells so good, so green, so alive. . ."

I was transfixed with the fullness of it all. This place was a realm of magic and movement, the air so sweet. Mesmerized, I wondered about spending a lifetime in a place like this, just watching the sunlight finding its way into the trees. In the midst of absolute perfection, I felt incredible peace inside. How could I preserve this feeling? I had no idea where I was or how I had gotten here, but perhaps I could persuade Daniel to let me stay here for a while.

Suddenly, my body went rapidly backwards and I caught my breath in time to see the tiny green thing under my nose. I was back in the field, crouched on my knees. Beside me was the familiar laughter.

"Isn't it good to see?" the boy asked, his arms outstretched to call attention to his point.

"What. . . what was that?" I gasped, heart trying to beat a path out of my chest. "Where was I?"

"Inside the fern, silly!" he replied with a grin. "Where did you think you were?" Not waiting for my stunned expression to make room for an answer, off he went through the field in search of other treasures.

"Wait!" I scrambled after him, being inordinately careful not to step on that little fern. "Wait. . . Daniel, just a minute. You can't just tell me I've been inside a plant and then walk off. . . wait! How did you do that?"

"Helped you drop your density. . . that's all," he said happily. "Like I keep telling you, the only reason you don't have all your abilities is 'cause you keep building up mud." He skipped a few steps, turned himself all the way around and then, seeing a new desire to learn burning within me, stopped.

"Look around. What do you see?" He sounded excited and I did as I was told.

"Well, I see lots of flowers and trees, some grass, a few boulders and some birds."

"Look again," he commanded. "This time, pay attention to the fact that they're all the same thing."

Confusion mingled with my already muddled mind, "I don't understand."

"Just go ahead," he encouraged. "See what you can see."

Gazing out over the field with this strange idea floating in my head, I tried to consider how trees and boulders and birds could possibly be the same thing? I looked around more carefully. There was something about this place, a pulsing quality, like the soft breath of a sleeping kitten.

Staring at a large, gray-speckeled rock, I tried to see what was strange. It seemed very happy. Happy was the perfect word, yet I felt ridiculous thinking it. How could a rock be happy? But then, everything I was seeing looked happy. Actually, it all looked joyful.

"Just keep looking, Rick. You'll see."

The little boy at my side sounded so confident and encouraging. As I fixed my attention on the rock, determined to experience whatever Daniel was talking about, it changed dramatically. For a fraction of a second, I could see inside it. Like an incandescent newspaper photograph, the rock was made up of tiny, sparkling particles of light vibrating in empty space.

"Daniel!" I said excitedly. "I could see inside that rock! I could see light inside that rock."

"Try looking at that bush," he advised quietly.

My mind rapidly assessed the object in front of me. "O.K., it's some kind of shrubby pine, doing quite well, would do better with more water."

Daniel's small voice chastised me gently, "You need to just look, Rick. Don't name it or judge it, just see what it is."

It suddenly occurred to me that I might be able to see energy moving in the pine, too. As soon as I allowed for the possibility, the little bush revealed itself. Scarcely willing to take in a breath, I desperately wanted to continue to see particles of light glittering before my eyes.

"That's it. See, I knew you could do it!" I heard the enthusiastic little voice beside me.

This was incredible. Of course, I knew about atoms and electrons, molecules, elementary physics. Since high school, I had known intellectually that everything was made up of these tiny, ever moving particles of energy. But to see it! How could a human being see these things without a machine?

Daniel looked up at me and quietly asked a startling question, "How do you think anyone ever figured out they needed to invent a machine that could see the energy?"

"Well, they just progressed along with the scientific method until a machine was needed and they built one." Although what I had said was certainly logical, I knew deep inside it was wrong.

Science. . . we're all taught that it's the ultimate in man's ability to reason. The scientific method is the only acceptable route to true knowledge. I remembered my statistics professor sarcastically comparing research based on mathematical computations with research based on interviewing actual people. I had learned then what people perceived was never reliable; a carefully constructed experiment, now that was valuable.

The little boy interrupted my ruminations, "Actually, they already knew what they built the machine to find out. They just built the machine because they forgot exactly how to see it without one." His words were matter of fact, but they shocked me.

"What do you mean, they already knew?" I cried. "How could they know? That's what science is all about. . . venturing into the unknown, forging ahead, building higher and higher on top of what we discover?"

"Well, science is like that, but it's the long way to go about it," he said as if it should be perfectly obvious. "Besides, even science doesn't always work that way. Think about what happens sometimes. A whole way of understanding something, even one that came straight out of science, gets totally thrown out and a new thing turns out to be more true! It isn't just collecting facts and building on them, is it?"

Well, he had a point, now that I thought about it. "You mean like Einstein changing the way we think about energy and matter?"

"Yep," he replied with a grin. "Now, didn't all the scientists up to then think they were doing a great job? And they were doing wonderfully at collecting facts, but the truth was bigger than the facts. And, what was different about Einstein?"

The reality of what he was saying acted like a depth charge in my stomach. "He was willing to look past what everyone else was seeing?"

"Right!" The little boy beamed, "He was willing to look inside to what he knew was true."

I breathed out my next words with amazement, "He knew that stuff all the time! He didn't discover it by objective research?" Albert Einstein was an icon, a scientific saint, our best example of the intellectual mind at work and it turned out he wasn't "scientific" at all!

"Yep," he nodded. "All the fact collecting and machines, it's just what people have to do because they've forgotten what they already know. If they would include themselves in their studies, they would know what they forgot a lot faster. But your whole scientific method is based on removing the person who already knows what they are wanting to know!" He giggled at the paradox and watched me continue to be amazed at my experience.

The little pine still had spaces in it. I slowly shifted my attention to a nearby tree. It was spacious too. "Daniel, I think I've got it down. I can see the spaces in the pine, the boulder and the tree!" I was so proud of myself.

"O.K., now look at yourself," he said. Suddenly, I was frightened. I didn't really want to see spaces in myself. I liked being a solid human being. The idea of being able to watch my own particulate matter roam around was unsettling, to say the least.

"It's all right, Rick," he said softly. "You can do it. You're only giving up an idea of what you are. Nothing will change except your awareness of what is real."

What did that mean? Of course I was real. . . but maybe I was real in a different way than I had thought. After all, I had gotten out of an airplane mid-flight without dying and I had just journeyed to the inside of a fern. I looked down. . . legs, arms, stomach, chest they were all there and they were all different. I was full of moving dots of energy, just like the boulder, tree and bush!

But there was something terribly alarming about what I was seeing. "Daniel, look at me! I'm so empty. . . there's so much empty space in here! Is this O.K.? Is this the way I'm supposed to look?"

"Oh Rick, don't you see?" he exclaimed. "Spinning atoms whirling in space is what you see as matter. But your body is only one percent matter and ninety-nine percent empty space. Who do you suppose lives in all that empty space?"

"Me?" I said lamely, hardly able to comprehend what he was saying.

"Of course it's you, silly!" he laughed. "You organize the matter and tell it how to spin. The intelligence that creates your body lives in the darkness between the atoms. Don't look at yourself as the one percent, when you're really so much bigger than that!"

"That's what you were trying to tell me about density. . ." I suddenly lost track of the thought which had seemed crystal clear a nanosecond ago.

Daniel smiled softly and said, "See, if you think you're just a thick, heavy, machine-like thing, then you make a world which compliments that perfectly. And if you see that you are a being of energy which will respond to what you want it to do, a reality is created that matches that. It's your own choice." He shrugged his shoulders, "But you guys have gotten so mixed up, you don't realize you have a choice any more."

Afraid to sound crazy, I whispered my question, "Are you telling me it's all what we create?"

"Yep," he said simply. "And most of what you produce is so dense, it takes the density of the physical body to meet it and move it around. What you call 'reality' is filled with density, something so thick, you can actually encounter it by just using your physical senses."

He surveyed my dazed expression and continued, "See, when you define yourself as dense, then what you see as 'reality' will be equally dense. Then, you make sure it stays that way by telling yourself things like, 'I've got to face reality!' All that means is that you command yourself to stay dense so you can move around all the density you create."

I felt trapped in a strange space in which my mind would simply not work. The little boy watched me struggle and then abruptly said, "Here, come over to this tree." Taking my hand, he carefully placed my palm against the smooth bark of a beautiful red maple. "See, when your hand is hard and dense, then the tree is, too." He lifted my hand away from the tree. "Now, see your hand the way it really is. . . just like you saw your body a moment ago."

Finding nowhere to hide, I focused on what I had learned. Closing my eyes for a moment, I practiced the idea that my body was not really the solid thing it appeared to be; I was spacious, not thick. I was energy in the form of a physical body. My eyes flew open as my hand suddenly gave way to sparkling particles.

"Now, put your hand back on the tree," he said quietly.

I followed his direction and found the tree was no longer solid either. When I touched it, I could stay on its surface, or move my hand right through it! I looked at him with a big smile.

"Now, is the tree real?" His question was light.

Overwhelmed by my magical experience, I replied, "Of course the tree is real, but not the way we've always seen it!"

He considered my new found ability and said, "For what you just did, you have to have intent."

"Intent?" I promptly found myself patting a tree which was again terribly solid.

"Yep," he shrugged. "See if you want something to happen on an energy level, you need to focus your awareness and truly decide that's what you want. If it is, that's it."

Some part of me was appalled at what I had just heard, "Daniel, how could that be? Isn't that just wishful thinking? Pretending? Denying reality?"

This child's concepts were directly opposed to everything I had ever learned: "You have to face reality." "Work hard and overcome the obstacles." "Keep your feet on the ground." "Don't be a dreamer." These ideas had been pounded into my head by the school system, my parents, the Boy Scouts, professors, friends. It seemed especially important as a man to obey these precepts.

After all, above everything, a man was supposed to be pragmatic, level-headed. It sounded terribly stereotypical to say that, but nonetheless that's the way it had always felt to me. Men who came up with big ideas but never met the bottom line were an embarrassment. I hadn't missed the men's movement. I knew all about the importance of feelings and the right to break out of traditional male patterns. Still, a man was expected to be responsible, trustworthy and strong, even if he did want to beat a drum on the weekends.

The little boy interrupted my thoughts, "Did you put your hand through that tree with a wish?"

"Well, no," I said, feeling utterly confused. After all, I couldn't argue with my experience. I had put my hand straight through an object which had always seemed solid.

Daniel had a smile on his face as he witnessed my continuing discomfort. "Well, how did you do it?" he prompted.

My mind was in a battle with itself that could rival anything that happened in the Civil War. Internal armies charged that what I had just accomplished was totally impossible. And yet, I had done it! I decided to simply repeat what Daniel had taught me until I could bring peace to the personal warfare. "I changed the way I saw myself and by doing so, I was able to see the tree."

He would not let me off the hook so easily. "Is there a difference between that and wishful thinking?"

I replied uneasily, "Well, one has to do with sitting around wishing things were different and the other with actually doing something different." Then my mind sent up a real defense, "But what about reality, Daniel? We all have to deal with certain things."

"Why?" he answered innocently.

I could feel the voices of every parent I had ever known coming up within me. "Because they're there, that's all. Certain things exist and we have to deal with them. Everybody knows that!"

"Why?" he repeated with a maddening grin.

I responded irritably, "Daniel! Because it's there."

"Why is it there?" He looked at me blankly and I wrestled inside with my frustration. What did he want me to say, "no, it's not there?"

"Daniel, it's there because it's there." I made my statement with the same tone of finality my high school gym teacher had used when he told me I was to keep running laps until he told me to stop.

"Like a body which absolutely must have an airplane to fly? Like trees and bushes and boulders are hard and unmoving?" His face was gentle again and he stopped and I felt his compassionate support while I allowed his words to blow me apart.

My last vestige of security gave way, accompanied by the sensation of a serious drop in blood pressure. "Daniel," I said weakly, "how can we ever know what is true?"

"Well," he looked up into the sky. "The truth is very simple and the confusion is very complicated. That's one way. See, it's what I've been trying to tell you. You just need to remember who you really are. It's very simple."

"Where do I even begin?" How could I dismantle the concepts which provided the girding under my mind?

"Well, you have to always remember something really important." He waited for me to ask what it was.

Predictably, I could not keep quiet for long, "What? What should I keep in mind?"

"That nothing, absolutely nothing is as it appears to be. . . even when you are certain." He smiled broadly and added, "Maybe I should say especially when you are certain."

I felt puzzled. "But what do I do differently?"

"You can start by making new choices." Seeing my continued confusion, he added, "Everything you do either increases or decreases your density. Look at the food you eat, is it dead or full of chemicals? Just like the plant you saw, your body wants to take in beautiful, life giving energy. Look at the places you spend time in. . . are they full of concrete and noise? Everything is made out of energy. . . find the places which are still alive."

He watched my uncertainty begin to lift and went on with renewed enthusiasm, "Look at who you spend time with. Are they filled with anger and heaviness? Do you feel burdened down after you've been around them? Look at how you live. What things can you let go of? Can you allow yourself to stop being busy and only do what's really important? Think about what movies you see, do images of violence and destruction really contribute anything but more energies of density?"

I considered what he had told me very carefully and then said soberly, "All those rules. . . I don't want to live like a monk, Daniel."

"Well, you know everything's free will!" he replied with a grin. "And they're not rules, just suggestions. See, that's how teaching gets distorted! Like your Ten Commandments, they were never meant as commandments, just suggestions about how you can set down density."

"Daniel. . ." I was momentarily caught in my own laughter, "the Ten Suggestions?"

"Yep," he replied with a nod. "Just some good ideas for you about staying free of density. They were never meant to be rules. And there's nobody out there ready to punish you if you don't follow them. The only thing is, you suffer in your own thickness if you make a choice to pick more density up."

His demeanor changed and his voice softened. Very gently he said, "You might want to think about whether what you have is really what you want deep inside. Rick, when it's three o'clock in the morning, that ache you sometimes feel in the middle of your chest. . . could it be that there really aren't enough things or projects in the world to solve that pain?"

How did he know about my three a.m. blues? When it was dark and silent, sometimes I had wondered if what I had was really all there was to life. I mean, you spend a lot of time trying to be successful. It seems like the most important thing you can do for yourself and your family. But after you have the nice house and the great stuff. . . well, there was a certain emptiness. When it came to your last few breaths, would it really matter what kind of car was parked out in the driveway?

I did not bother to deny the feelings I sometimes had, "What's density got to do with that ache, Daniel?"

"It keeps you separate. . . that's the main thing," he answered sadly. "It makes you forget how everything's all connected. That ache is really about suffering from an awful loneliness." He watched me carefully, "Somewhere inside, you know you've been cut off from something really important. Once you begin to be cut off, you kind of close up and start to get thick. . . then you get scared."

I did not want that to be true of me. I scurried to find a way to make it personally inapplicable. "But, I have a great relationship. We share everything. We're very close. . . " Despite my effort, I already knew that's not what he meant.

"That's part of the confusion!" he said and then saw that I needed no further argument. Tenderly, he continued to try to help me understand, "See, when you're cut off from all the connectedness, you have to attach yourself to other people and try to substitute them for what you really need. It's like. . . well, it's like if you were by a beautiful, clear lake that offered all the water you could ever need for anything, but you forgot it was there and you started to die. If somebody came by with even a thimble full of water, you'd think they were the most important thing in the world. Pretty soon, you'd be desperate to make sure they were always right there. You'd have to start figuring out ways to keep them around. That doesn't have much to do with love. . . not really." With that, he started walking again.

"Well, what are we supposed to be connected with?" I was feeling my frustration return as I followed him further into the land of who knows where. Suddenly, I had the answer! "Oh, I get it, that's why we need to find God!"

Pleased with my great accomplishment in understanding, I was dumbfounded when Daniel looked over at me, apparently exasperated.

"That's exactly how you all get lost!" he shouted. "How do we get you guys to give up looking into the sky for the answers? Those darn Earth gods, they really make it difficult. Things were a lot more hopeful before they came along. . . but density makes so many problems."

54

I slammed on my brakes and Daniel innocently inquired, "Why'd you stop? Come on, I want you to see."

"Wait a minute," I choked. "Did you say something about 'Earth gods'. . . what does that mean? You said, 'gods', plural. . . and Earth. . . isn't God in charge of it all? What do you mean, the Earth gods came along?"

He heaved a huge sigh and said with consternation, "Well, just look."

I really did not like that phrase. Every time Daniel said those words, something really difficult was about to happen. Nevertheless, I looked out past his outstretched finger and promptly quit breathing.

Chapter 12

We were well beyond the Earth, but I could see the vibrant blue sphere turning in the blackness, beautiful as ever. But now, there were four enormous, male figures surrounding it. Jostling for territory, each appeared several times larger than the Earth.

Astounded by the sight, I managed to whisper, "What the hell is that?"

Daniel looked across the cosmos and, disgust thick in his voice answered, "That's them, the Earth gods. . . all four of them. You know, Yahweh, Jehovah, the evil one and the nameless, faceless one."

"Daniel. . . Yahweh and Jehovah. . . that's God in the Bible. . . the evil one, that's what some people call Satan. . . " I trailed off, terrified to hear his answer.

"Yep. . . and the nameless, faceless one is what lots of other religions think of as God," he replied.

Seeing my shocked expression, he continued, "Pretty scary things to create, don't you think? That's density for you. . . makes ugly stuff."

"What's that coming out from the Earth?" I managed to choke out my question, afraid the God of my childhood would turn and dismiss my existence with a thought.

"That's all the energy of the human beings going up to feed the Earth gods," he said sadly. "See, they can't even exist unless you guys continue to give up your own power. The people of Earth created them and keep them going every time they look up into the air and outside of themselves for instructions and help."

His little arms were crossed over his chest and he looked intensely serious for a change. We stood together and watched the steady streams of energy flooding out and upward from the Earth. These Earth gods did not stand passively, but fought to catch the resources being sent. At the moment, it appeared to me that Jehovah was winning, but the evil one seemed almost as strong.

"What's that foggy looking thing out to the side," I asked, watching an amorphous figure drift just beyond the range of the four competitors.

"Oh, that's the new one," he replied, a hint of sarcasm in his voice. "People have created another Earth god for themselves. They call it 'the light,' but it's just the most recent invention of something outside they can look to."

Seeing my confusion, he added, "Some people started to know about how God must be different than they had been taught. They turned away from the old ideas, but they just ended up making another Earth god. The other ones think it's funny, you know humans believing they can get away from them. They just call the new god their little sister. She just helps to keep the truth from being known and the energy keeps coming up to feed them."

"Daniel, is there any hope for us?" I said desperately. "I thought 'the light' was a positive thing, something apart from religious institutions. What's wrong with that?"

"It could have been good." He shrugged his shoulders, "But see, people are just turning it into another god in the sky. The only difference is they don't think about this one as being like a human, you know, gray beard and robes and stuff. But, it's still outside the person somewhere and it's still more powerful and it still requires that the person turn to it for help."

Suddenly, Daniel's hands flew up past his head and out to the sides. "Let them go," he shouted. "Just leave them alone. Leave those people alone!"

I had nowhere to hide. Daniel was yelling at God and I had nowhere to hide. All I could see were silver stars suspended in the blackness. There was nowhere to go and nothing to do, but wait for the inevitable repercussions of his careless actions.

What happens to you if God decides to wipe you out? But which god? There were four, almost five of them out here. There was only supposed to be one God! And I could see the energy from Earth, so astoundingly beautiful, transparent, shimmering energy, sent out into the control of four. . . five. . . five shams, five phonies, five actors with the Earth in their hands.

None of them was paying the slightest bit of attention to the little boy's outburst. "Daniel, why aren't they responding to you?"

"Because they know perfectly well that Earth is a planet of free will," he answered angrily. "They don't have anything to worry about as long as the people there continue to make the decision to feed them. You know, if people would just stop, those guys would be gone instantly, but we can't do anything about it."

The existence of these powerful, destructive creatures was clearly a terrible tragedy for us all. I asked, "How did they get started? Where did they come from in the first place?"

"Power and confusion... simple as that," he answered, shaking his head. "When you started to get confused, other people started taking advantage of that confusion. They had lost track of who they really are too, but you didn't know that."

I looked at him blankly. "Who are you talking about?"

Taking a breath he said, "You know, your religious leaders. I like to call them keepers of the buildings, 'cause they do a really good job of taking care of pretty buildings and an awful job of reminding you about who you really are."

It was beginning to occur to me our religious leaders might not know any more than we did about the reality of these Earth gods. I dared to ask my question, "Daniel, do they know the answer? Do they know who we really are?"

"By now, most of them have forgotten completely," he said sadly.

Watching my reaction, he added, "But the thing is, nobody knows they don't know what they seem to. I mean, mostly, people think ministers and priests have some kind of special connection to God that they don't have. But secretly, most of the keepers know they don't have any connection at all. They can't admit that or they'd lose their position and their power."

I was about to ask him if anybody on Earth knew the answers when he continued, "Sometimes, there are people who do know more, but a lot of them decide not to tell 'cause people wouldn't need them any more."

Suddenly, we were in a room somewhere, it felt like a long time ago. I could see several robed figures sitting in a circle. They looked like priests of some kind. It was cold here and looked like it had always been damp, the rain falling continuously, feeding the dusky mold creeping its way across the stone.

"They can't hear you or see you," Daniel said softly. Somehow, I was aware of being able to perceive more than the words being spoken.

"The people must never have this." The words came quietly, the air barely disturbed. Meeting in daylight under images meticulously constructed, they held no fear of being seen. There was no need for emphasis, each man in the circle felt the message hit hard in his solar plexus.

"It would mean the end of everything." Like the wind touching weeds in a field, their heads nodded silently in agreement. Under the subtle glow of gemstones and the flicker of gold, their hearts were cold. Their people were terrified and that was good.

"How can we contain this?" One spoke uneasily, his robe registering a shift in rigid posture. "It almost seems destined to become known." He bowed his dark head unwilling to meet the judgmental eyes, frightened the others might think him disloyal. Retribution could come swiftly.

"We will do what is necessary. We must give them a story they can accept and hide the rest. No one would dare question us." The man looked at the others, hoping to find in them the courage he only pretended to hold.

"How long. . . ?" The white hands glistened with moisture sent up by fear. Twisting, the fingers ground against each other with anxiety. "How long will we have?" The voice trembled and the man shook.

"Perhaps forever," a stronger note sounded. "It will all be ours. After all, who among them will ever ask?"

"Daniel. . . Daniel," I whispered, afraid of being seen.

He spoke at full volume, "Don't worry, remember they can't hear you or see you."

"Who are these people?" I asked, shocked by what I had heard. "They're horrible. . . mean-spirited. What are they trying to hide?"

He replied sadly, "Just what is most important in the whole world. . . who you really are. It doesn't matter who they are. There have been people like this all along, all over your world, in all the different religions, all wanting to confuse you and weaken you so they could have the power."

I grasped for hope, "What about all the spiritual teachers on Earth right now? It seems like a whole host of them all of a sudden. Isn't that a positive thing?"

"Looking for spiritual guidance can be a dangerous thing," he answered. "See, a teacher should only help you to remember for yourself. If they're telling you what to do and how to think, they're only keepers."

"How in the world can we ever figure out what's true?" My head was pounding. This was too much for me to sort out by myself. Even though I had not personally figured out the answers to life's greatest mysteries, I always thought it was because I didn't devote enough time and attention to studying the classics, philosophy, Greek, Hebrew, something.

Everybody has a Bible, few people read it, so you decide someday you will and then you'll understand the important things. Or the Talmud, the Koran, whatever. I always thought it was a matter of being disciplined enough to study the right things. Wasn't that what religious leaders were supposed to be doing?

I drew up what remained of the courage within me. "Daniel. . . if what we thought was God isn't really God, what the hell is it?"

"A really dangerous distraction," he replied quietly. "As long as people stay focused on that, they'll never remember."

Unwilling to rest peacefully, my mind went into overdrive and thoughts began to ricochet in my head. "Daniel, are you telling me the words of all our great teachers have been mixed up? You mean, we all learned garbled messages about what God is and what we are?"

"Yep," he replied, eyes unflinching.

His answer was at once so simple and so thoroughly complete, I was stopped for a moment. The whole thing was mind boggling. Getting off an airplane mid-flight was easy compared to entertaining the idea that what I had always thought was God was only something birthed into reality by the misguided actions of man. Our own fear and confusion had jelled into a being that terrified us. We gave him life and then fell to our knees and begged his forgiveness!

"Daniel, what you've told me is blasphemy!" I felt a rush of fear, familiar as it was painful. "Don't think in ways that would offend God out there." "Don't do things that will cause him to punish you." "Never offend him or a zap of lightening will certainly shoot from the sky and send you straight to hell." I shuddered, thinking about all the threats of damnation in the Bible. But, was that just manufactured to scare us all to death? What better way to stop somebody from thinking things through!

"That's how it works, Rick," he said gently. "They make you afraid to question. If you don't look too hard, they can keep the power."

"Daniel," I cried, "this is nothing more than a giant dysfunctional family. . . you know, where everyone is so scared of a father who has rage attacks that nobody dares to question him. Each person becomes dedicated to not making dad angry. Everyone loses their freedom to be themselves because they're terrified about what dad might do!"

"It's an interesting comparison," he replied wryly.

Trembling, I waited for him to go on.

"Look at your New Testament," he shook his head sadly. "That's so horribly mixed up, I can hardly believe what happened sometimes!"

"Mixed up," I said weakly.

He seemed momentarily worried about my ability to handle more shocking information. Seeing I was still conscious, he went on, "The early writers, the ones who were there with Jesus, actually for many years after he left his body, tried to record the truth. People hurt them, even killed them sometimes. Then they took their words and changed them all around so a few people could have all the power. It's really not very hard to see how mixed up it is if you're not afraid to look."

"It isn't?" I was afraid of what he might say next. After all, he was bordering on saying the Bible was simply not true.

"Well, just look at what an awful story they tell you!" he said as though it should be perfectly obvious. "Why would a God of love willingly send his own son to suffer and to die in order to save the people from his own anger? Why wouldn't he just simply love and help them? Can you really accept the idea that God loves the son and loves the people so much that he kills one so he won't kill them all?" Daniel face reflected exasperation as he waited for my answer.

I had never thought about it like that! He was right, how could that story be true? And what about suffering? How could an almighty, loving God permit little children to die from horrible diseases? Why did floods and fires destroy life? That term, "An Act of God," had always puzzled me a little. I could never put it together with the words of some hollow eyed disaster survivor, "Everyone around us was killed, but God saved us. Our prayers were answered." What did that mean? God created the disaster in the first place and then allowed some people to perish while others were spared. What kind of a God was that? If a person acted that way, we'd lock him up as a psychopath.

I struggled to find some answer to my dilemma. "Some people believe God does all these things as a test of our love. . . you know, like Job."

"Rick," he said softly. "How could a God of love send terrible pain to see if you will still love him? The only thing that's created is fear, the opposite of love."

Looking at me with compassion, he went on, "You have lived for so long with the idea that if you displease some horrible being, he will send violent punishment down on you. But your keepers continue to tell you this has to do with love! You can see how much confusion there is."

My mind had caught on a particular point. "Wait a minute, you said something really interesting, Daniel. Isn't the opposite of love, hate?"

Shaking his head, he answered, "No Rick. . . it's fear. . . constriction and building up of walls of density. That keeps you separated and alone. Did you know that the word sin means to be apart from God, or to miss the mark? It has nothing to do with satisfying rules. Why would a loving God care about whether you follow a rule or not? Doesn't it seem awfully petty?"

My limbs felt numb, the beginning sign of shock and I nodded my head mutely in agreement as he went on. "See, what has been distorted into rules that have to be followed in order to avoid the wrath of a terrible God was only meant to help people see how they could set down density. It's your free will to set it down, through one kind of action, or pick it up through another. The punishment comes out of the kind of reality that you make when you create more density, not out of the judgment of a god."

I thought about a story I had used with clients who kept making the same mistakes over and over again. They often felt they were somehow mentally or morally defective after the fourth marriage or the tenth lost job. I would remind them results come from the actions they take. Therefore, if they didn't like the results they were getting in their lives, they needed to change the actions that were creating those results.

It had never occurred to me to look at the Bible or other spiritual teachings as sets of directions for creating reality. I always thought it was just "the truth," and it was me who was always falling short. I certainly didn't think to consider these words as directions for living, for building communities and nations. But that's what they were. Daniel was saying our directions were all mixed up. Even if we ever followed them exactly, they flat out couldn't work!

"What about Satan?" I offered weakly, knowing I was about to see the last of my common belief system fall completely apart.

"More mixed up teaching, I'm afraid," he confirmed. "See, Satan has come into reality because humans have made him. But he's just created out of density, the density inside people."

"Are you saying that it's not Satan who's got us, but density? That density is created by us and we use it to create Satan? If we get rid of the density, there he goes. . . off into oblivion!" That was a big relief. After all, that was always the back-up threat. . . if I didn't follow God's rules well enough, Satan was out there ready to get me.

"That's right," he answered, clearly glad I was able to grasp what he was telling me.

Daniel was saying we had created our God out of our own energy! Once we got him started, he took on a life of his own. All over the world, everyone had done the same thing, creating different gods out of different misunderstandings. Now, those gods were out there influencing our lives, hurting us, creating fear and controlling us. And through our fear and ignorance, we continued to provide the energy to sustain them!

All the teachings were mixed up, garbled, confused beyond recognition. It wasn't laziness about spiritual obedience that had the world in this mess, but relying on totally scrambled messages. We had been doing the best we could with faulty information.

No wonder so many people just gave up. People were leaving churches in droves. People were depressed, alienated, lost out there. We were telling each other we were having a tough time because we didn't work hard enough and didn't follow the rules. Meanwhile, we were all lost and didn't know it!

And nobody knew! Not even the spiritual experts. They didn't understand any better than the rest of us. They inherited the same confusion and made institutions out of their misunderstanding. They kept these Earth gods going by giving them power, by worrying about ways to please them, by looking up into the heavens for answers.

All everybody had done was create Earth gods, make up rules and play a terrible game of pretend! If mankind had derailed along the way, it had better get back on track fast. Our adherence to a bunch of garbled messages had led to destruction. Earth's people were violent, diseased, hungry and demoralized.

"Daniel, this is a tragedy, an awful series of catastrophic mistakes!" I held the sides of my head, trying to contain the truth quickly multiplying past the confines of my skull.

Silently, he nodded his agreement.

A phrase from my old Sunday school days went through my mind, "By its fruits you shall know it. . ." All the mixed up teachings had born was anguish, fear and violence. Western civilization had been built on the Bible. Other parts of the world were busy following equally confused documents with tragic results. Tears rolled down my face as the enormity of our mistakes swept over me like an unexpected big wave at the seashore.

He looked at me, sorrow filling his eyes and said, "See, while people are busy falling to their knees and calling to their gods, they forget about the work they have to do. I'm so afraid if you don't begin to make choices to get rid of the density, your Earth will die."

Chapter 13

The scent of flowers whispered across my face and I found myself standing back in the field. The child who always seemed to be ahead of me was walking away. Scrambling after him, I called out, "The Earth may die! Daniel, isn't that a little strong? I mean, I know we aren't taking care of our resources very well and that pollution is pretty bad, but die?"

I considered myself an environmentalist. After all, it didn't take a rocket scientist to realize that Earth had finite resources and we'd better start taking good care of them. I lived in Idaho, after all. Even in my own lifetime, I had been witness to a terrible decline in the salmon population. People didn't seem to understand that we have to be careful about how we use the Earth so that the beauty could be enjoyed by everyone forever. . . but "die." That sounded suspiciously like something a radical would say. You know, a "make the trees more important than the people," kind of a statement. I couldn't go that far. After all, we were entitled to use the resources of the Earth. . . that's what it was there for.

The little boy stopped and turned to me, "Yes, Rick. Die. See with all of the increases in density, the Earth just can't support you. She was perfectly capable of taking care of you if you continued to set it down. . . but all these increases. . . it's not her fault, you know."

"Her. . . you mean Mother Nature. . . Mother Earth?" Somewhere inside me, I knew his response was going to be difficult.

"No, her. . . her, you know, Gaia," he said as if I should know this information already. "When she came from heaven and built a body to support all of you, she had no idea you were going to make the choices you made. It's really not fair, you know. I'm not sure she ever would have volunteered for this if she had. . ."

I remember the exact moment when I lost my mind. Somehow, it just fell apart like the roses in my wife's garden. At a certain point, the petals begin to fall, one by one until there's nothing left. I could see Daniel's mouth moving. I could hear sounds, but they no longer made sense until he started calling my name.

"Rick. . . Rick. . ." His little face reflected concern. "I'm sorry. I went too fast. They warned me about that. . . don't tell him too much. Human beings can't take it. They want to know, but they can't take it. It's like. . . well, we have an ocean to give you, but you only have a glass to take it with. Are you O.K.?"

My legs made an independent decision to let me fall to the ground. We were on a little slope, the air was warm and perfectly clear while the birds rhapsodized in the tall trees. I allowed myself to sink into the soft, emerald grass and looked over at the little boy with amazement. He was concerned, forehead furrowed and eyes intent.

"Are you O.K.?" he repeated with his child voice. I did not know how to answer him. What did "O.K." mean any more?

I felt somehow innocent, stripped of the beliefs which normally bound my being. I was no longer interested in being courageous, strong, intellectual or even particularly grownup. "Such as a little child shall enter the kingdom of heaven. . ." as the words rang in my head, they made sense to me for the first time.

"Daniel. . ." I whispered. "Can we just stay here for a little while? I mean, could we not blip off to somewhere else for a few minutes?"

"Sure!" he said enthusiastically. And then he vanished.

Too tired to be alarmed, I was grateful he had left me on firm ground this time. I stretched out and felt the fragrant Earth send comforting arms up to meet me. I let go, just let go. . . for once in my life, I just let it all go.

I heard a voice off to my right somewhere. Drifting comfortably, I chose not to open my eyes. She seemed quite content to talk without my attention. Vaguely, I wondered if Daniel was coming back and let myself float up and down on the current of her words. . .

"You see, Rick, you were all lost long ago and Gaia came to help you. Earth is not a solid lump of rock, but a living being with a body designed to nourish and sustain you. Just as you have a physical body inhabited by a spiritual being, so does Earth. Just look. . ."

I was having the most wondrous dream. A luminescent woman stood in front of me. Although she was very beautiful, it was her song that compelled me. A beautiful humming sound came from her and entered through my skin, traveled through all of my organs and landed softly in my heart where it seemed to explode in a thousand voices of love. I cried for the beauty of it. She reached out and I went toward her knowing she had a gift for me. She opened her hands and there it was, Earth. So blue, so impossibly exquisite, it turned slowly. I could see particles of light flowing freely within this sphere; beautiful, sparkling light, unencumbered, increasing as I watched.

"Come home, Rick. . . please, come home. . ." she sang softly to me as I continued to bask in her love.

"Going back to rejoin all the other beings is your right; there is a place where you belong and where in your absence the rest grieve. . . for each must be home for home to be home. Each of you cannot remain lost for home to be home. Each of you has a place, a seat, if you will, that shall remain empty until you arrive. And each of you is waited for with all the love of the whole. And each of you is called. . . and sung to. . . and held. . . and sheltered. . . and wished for with all the heart. There is no being among you who is disposable. . . no being among you who can truly be lost and not missed, for without you we are not whole. Do not think, 'I do not matter,' for you matter as much as the totality of all itself."

I was awakened by my own sobs. I turned over onto the warm Earth and let myself continue to cry. From deep inside me, I knew I had not experienced a dream, but the truth. And in that moment, I cried for us all. Belly heaving against Gaia's body, I gave my tears to her, not knowing what else I could do.

Chapter 14

"Time to get up! Come on. . . you get to be the one. . . you get to see. . . and I get to come, too!" I heard the voice calling to me from far away. He sounded so excited. How could anyone be so happy at this point?

"Daniel?" My eyes felt permanently stuck together and my mind judged that as a good state of affairs. I was afraid to open them, unsure I could take any more. Cracking one eye, I found his small face inches from mine.

"Hi," he said simply.

Surprised at his latest intrusion on social distance, I quickly pushed myself back and and sat up. "Why do you do these things?"

It was a rhetorical question. By now, I knew perfectly well why he did these things; he liked to shock me, keep me off guard. It was as simple as that.

I needed some time to sort things out and when he took my hand as if to pull me to my feet I cried, "Stop! Just wait a minute!" My head hurt. A tremendous pounding sent shards of pain straight through my scalp. "Let me ask some questions here. . . there's just been too much for me to take in."

He grinned back at me. "It's not so hard to understand. It's just like I said, everybody on the Earth gets here and then they forget and it takes them forever to remember and in the meantime, the Earth can't take it any more and. . ."

"Wait. Just wait a second. Let me just stop and think." I shook my head slightly to one side, as though the motion might settle my brain cells in a more comfortable position. "Daniel. . . the Earth. . . Gaia. . . it's, she's alive? Was that real? What I saw, was that real?"

Looking over at me, his smile of affirmation was like the sun coming up. "Daniel, just who are you anyway?"

"That's not important at all, silly!" he laughed. "The real question is, who are you?"

I decided to try to give a concise statement about what I had gathered thus far. "Well, from what I can figure out, I'm a human being who is terribly confused about himself, the world and the nature of reality, just like the rest of the people on Earth."

"That's good!" Daniel piped up with encouragement.

"Confusion is good?" Another of my common sense rules was about to go out the window.

"It is a good start," he said with his usual, utterly maddening good humor. "Confusion is the first sign of letting go of something you always thought was absolute truth."

It's also the first sign of mental illness, Alzheimer's and a lot of other terrible things, I thought silently. My head was pounding.

"Would you like me to fix your headache?" my companion asked brightly.

"That'd be great," I said, vainly pushing against my temples. "I would appreciate some aspirin. I can't concentrate with this pain."

He placed his small hands on my head and whispered, "Just let me be with you. Just let me come in."

He was so gentle, I closed my eyes and momentarily forgot to hold on to my fear. Why not let down my defenses with him? My world had already come unglued. What more could he do to me?

"That's it. Just let go." I relaxed into my heart and knew I was safe. Instantly, my headache went away.

My eyes flew open. "How did you do that!"

He shrugged and replied, "Just helped you again with your density. You were just scared about all the stuff you've been learning and you fell right back in the mud."

"And that gave me a headache?" I asked, surprised density had anything to do with physical pain.

He said matter of factly, "Any time you get sick it's always because of density, you know. Your energy gets all divided up, like I was telling you before. When that happens, parts of your body start to suffocate. . . just like when air gets cut off and you can't breathe. When parts of your body are cut off from energy, they start to hurt and sometimes they even start to die off.''

What he said made sense to me, but I knew our medical system had no idea about density. Reading my mind, Daniel responded, "The thing is, your doctors are great at following what happens to people's bodies while they suffocate from density. But they don't know a thing about how a body can get better when the person decides to free it up from all that thickness!''

He laughed ruefully, "You know what? A lot of times, doctors don't have any idea why something they give to a sick person works. They are really surprised when the person gets better. It's a good thing they don't want anybody to know they don't know what happened. . . if the doctor acts surprised, the person can get sick all over again just because he falls back into density. . . you know, the kind of density that has to do with fear and doubt.''

"Are you saying people cure themselves?" I asked, half hoping it was true. After all, if density could make us sick, then knowing about it could make us well again.

He continued, "Well, lots of people get better even if the doctor just gives them sugar pills. . . that's really important 'cause it shows how people heal themselves when they get their energy flowing by going past the fear and believing they will get better. I think that's really important, don't you?''

I had never thought about it like that. Why did we so easily dismiss apparent healing of the physical body in response to an inert substance as "merely the placebo effect." After all, the person did get well somehow. Like that term "spontaneous remission." What exactly did that mean? Daniel was saying that people healed themselves when they believed they were going to get better. Furthermore, he said that had to do with density and energy flow.

What had happened seemed to be so utterly simple. My pain was totally gone. "Daniel. . . my head really does feel completely better. Tell me some more about how energy and healing go together.''

"O.K." he agreed and then fumbled for a good way to explain it to me. "Well, let's see. . . it's kind of hard to explain. . . it's like this. . . no, that's not a good example. . . well. . . let's see, no. . . oh, just look!''

Chapter 15

My eyes had involuntarily closed. Like Pavlov's famous dogs, I had learned my lessons very well. The words, "just look" had come to mean something radical was about to occur. In this moment, I was entirely sure I was not up to dealing with whatever it was.

The little boy's voice sounded suspiciously cheerful, "Rick. . . Rick. . . come on. . . open your eyes! You can do it. I want you to see!"

It was dark here. Completely black. "Daniel. . . " My voice was shaking and I was deeply afraid at the thought he might not be by my side. "Daniel. . . are you there?"

"Of course I'm here. Where else would I be?" He asked the question with a tone that implied he had been unfailingly by my side.

"Where are we?" I asked quietly, barely willing to turn my head.

"It's really something, don't you think?" The merry voice seemed incongruous with the setting. This place seemed terribly serious. I had never been especially afraid of the dark, but this was so completely silent and black, so devoid of anything.

I looked up in time to see a bright light coming straight at us. "Look out!" I cried, ducking as a sphere about the size of a basketball flew past at rapid speed.

"Pretty wonderful, don't you think?" Daniel said enthusiastically.

"How can you say that?" I demanded, carefully surveying the horizon for another dangerous. . . another dangerous. . . what the hell was that?

"Here comes another one," Daniel said quietly. "Isn't it beautiful?"

Terrified, I looked out across the darkness and saw nothing. "I don't see anything, Dan. . ." I fell to my knees as the ball of light came toward me faster than anything I had ever seen.

Panic coursed through my body. "Daniel. . . please help me. Where are we? I want out of here." Hysteria was unbecoming, but imminently impossible to avoid. "Get me the hell out of this place."

He sounded very disappointed, "But, I want you to see. . . you said you wanted to understand about healing."

"Healing?" I choked out through clenched teeth. "Healing? Are you out of your mind?" I was glad I had remained on my knees as another spinning ball zoomed into view and headed right for us.

"Well, how are you going to know how to feel better if you don't understand this place?" He said calmly as the unidentified flying object went overhead.

"What are you talking about?" I did not want to debate with him and brought up my most commanding tone, "I'm telling you, get me the hell out of here, right now!"

"Rick. Try to calm down," he said softly. "Everything is perfectly all right. Just watch."

I didn't want to watch anything anymore at any time, ever again. Nonetheless, I knew my best chance to get out of this godforsaken place was to follow his instructions.

I could hear my breath coming and going like a wild animal caught in a cage. "O.K., O.K., I can't see anything. What do you want me to watch?"

"Watch the sphere," he said quietly. My heart lurched as another bright light appeared out of nowhere. "Don't panic this time. Just concentrate for a minute." The ball headed for us at supersonic speed.

"Concentrate! Concentrate on what?" I cried as I threw myself down.

"Well, concentrate on what you want it to do, of course," he replied as though telling me something perfectly obvious.

"I want it to stop," I screamed.

"Just concentrate, Rick," he repeated. "Tell it to stop."

"Stop! Stop! Stop!" I yelled, bringing every particle of strength I had into the command. The ball of light stopped.

"That's good!" Daniel said like a father whose second grader had managed finally to hit the baseball.

Suspended in the darkness, the sphere turned slowly, seemingly waiting for further instructions like a dog in obedience school.

"Well, what do you want it to do now?" Daniel asked brightly.

"I want it to go away," I said with a mixture of fatigue and desperation.

"So, tell it to go away," he instructed softly.

"Go away," I stated with little enthusiasm. Nothing happened. I looked over at Daniel with renewed fear. "What do I do now? It didn't work."

"Well, how can you expect anything to happen if you don't apply any feeling to what you say?" He asked, sounding quite frustrated with my inability to understand.

"What's feeling have to do with it?" I asked, watching the globe with the kind of wariness usually prompted by a bee making its way across the windshield of my car in afternoon traffic.

He heaved a big sigh and said, "How's he supposed to know what to pay attention to if you don't care about it?"

"He? He? The ball is a he?" My voice sounded like a rusty door hinge.

Daniel's laughter filled the silence, "Of course the ball isn't a he. . . I was talking about the guy who runs this place!"

Chapter 16

At last report, my mind had fallen apart like the spent petals of a rose. . . now, those petals spiraled chaotically down the street in a perilous, swift wind.

"Runs this place. . . ?" Struck silent, I was dumbfounded by the sight of a man appearing out of the darkness. Enormous, he held the still spinning ball of light in his hands. His azure eyes were luminous and calm and he looked at me as if waiting for something.

"Well. . . tell him what to do!" Daniel's voice seemed so very far away. This man was beautiful in his simplicity. Clear light seemed to shine from his face and those eyes were filled with devotion.

"I don't know what you mean," I whispered softly.

The child amplified his statement, "That's what he's waiting for. . . you know, for you to tell him what to do with the energy."

"You mean the ball. . . that's energy?" I said lamely.

"Well of course!" As an afterthought, he asked, "What did you think it was?"

I felt apologetic about my ignorance. "Daniel. . . please try to remember, I don't know anything. . . who is this person?" I looked again at this gentle face. . . it seemed he would do anything I asked.

"I'm sorry," Daniel bailed me out of my embarrassment. "I keep forgetting that you've forgotten everything. . . that's so weird how it works. . . why you forget and everything. . . personally, I think things would go a lot better if you remembered in the first place. Do you have any idea how much time gets wasted in this forgetting thing? I mean. . ."

"Daniel. . . please!" The giant man in front of me had reached out his hand and caught another globe of light. His eyes held renewed expectation.

I needed some answers, "Who is this man? Where are we? Why is he waiting for me to tell him what to do with the energy?"

"Well, who else would tell him?" Daniel sounded genuinely confused.

"Why me? I don't know him or anything about this place," I retorted, a little annoyed. The man was beginning to remind me of a Labrador retriever I had when I was about fifteen. The dog would sit at my feet and look up at me with absolute dedication and love. He would wait forever for one word, one pat on the head from me. That was a special kind of love.

With a measure of exasperation, the little boy threw out his arms and set off his bomb. "Rick. . . for heaven's sake. . . of course you have to tell him what to do. He belongs to you and so does that energy! How else could your body run?"

"Body? Did you say body?" I felt dizzy; what did this being have to do with my body?

"Well, where do you think we are, silly?" He looked at me innocently before continuing his challenge to my sensibilities. "We're inside your body! And that's your nature spirit. All human beings have one. When your body first starts up, you know, when you come to Earth you have to have a body to use while you're here. . . everybody knows that. Anyway, it's his job to construct the body and to keep it all running. He does that with energy. . . a special kind of energy that only nature spirit has!"

Stunned, I had no response to offer and he continued, "Isn't it good that you don't have to worry all the time about your heart beating and your food getting digested and all that stuff? That would really be a pain if you had to say, 'beat' for all 100,000 times your heart beats every twenty four hours! What if you had to tell yourself all the time to stay at 98.6 degrees? That would keep you up all night! And what if you had to worry about remembering to create all seven million new red blood cells that appear every second!

"People should be really grateful to their nature spirit. What would you do without him?" Daniel finished this astounding speech by pointing directly at the man in front of me. He had caught several more balls of light and continued to look patiently at me.

"I don't know what to tell him to do with that energy." I said weakly.

"Well," he said enthusiastically, "why don't you tell him to send it through your system freely and smoothly. . . then you won't be so tired! Of course, he's going to have to fight through the clutter of the density you've got going to do that, but ask anyway."

As if by immediate thought transference, as soon as I agreed to do as Daniel suggested, the man threw the spheres forward and spiraling beautifully, they disappeared from sight. I immediately felt a wave of energy sweep through me. Suddenly, I was invigorated and ready to understand more.

"All this time, I've had this nature spirit just waiting for me to tell him what to do with the energy?" My heart was pounding with excitement, "Where does the energy come from?"

Daniel shrugged and said, "That depends a lot on what you eat, the air you take in, the water you drink. . . when you eat animals, instead of giving you energy, nature spirit has to defend against the fear and anguish that comes in. . . did you know that? The way the animals die so that people can eat them, they are so afraid at the end. That energy is what you take in when you eat meat. And water, by the time you drink it, there are more chemicals than water in it. And air. . . besides all the pollution, most people don't seem to breathe. They take air in little short gasps, way high up in their chest. Watch them sometimes. See how many take a full breath all the way down into their belly."

Watching the beautiful man in front of me, I asked, "Does he listen all the time. . . I mean, about what we want him to do with the energy?"

"Of course he does!" Daniel answered. "See, he can't choose by himself. He loves you so much; he just waits for you to tell him. It's just, well, he's kind of simple. He gets confused a lot. I mean, if you keep repeating something, even if you don't really mean it, even if it hurts you in the end, he will do it because you told him to do it. So, you have to be careful about what you say."

I thought for a moment and asked, "How can we be careful if we don't even know he's there? Do you mean he listens to everything. . . all the time?"

"Yep," he nodded. "That's his job. . . run your body just the way you tell him to. So, watch out when you keep saying your job is a pain in the neck or your back is breaking. He even listens to things like people saying over and over that they aren't good enough or big enough to do things. I'm afraid he sometimes starts making lots more cells so they'll be enough. . .

you guys end up with what you call cancer. He doesn't mean to hurt you. It's just, like I said, he's kind of simple."

I continued to gaze at the incredible man in front of me. He had captured another two spheres and seemed once again to be waiting for me to tell him what to do. "Daniel, how does he know about making my heart beat without me telling him. . . I mean, I don't think I've ever even thought about it particularly, let alone asked for my heart to go ahead and beat."

"Oh," he replied. "He knows that from the basic pattern he got in the first place. You know, the one you gave him when you came here. . . tell him to send some of that energy he's holding through you. You still look a little tired."

"Tired! Tired! How in the world would you expect me to feel after all of this? Of course I'm tired!" I sounded exasperated.

He met my frustration with some of his own, "See, that's what I'm trying to tell you, people keep thinking they feel sick or tired because of stuff going on outside of themselves. But it's not about that at all. It's what you tell him to do with the energy and how much energy you give him to use by the choices you make. . . and of course, how much density you've got blocking your energy pathways. You can change it because you created it in the first place!"

"I did?" I said a little defensively.

"Well sure!" he answered. "Give your nature spirit a name. . . talk to him directly. Give him what he needs to do what you ask, and there you go, it's yours for the asking!"

The man was so beautiful, incandescent, almost transparent, his eyes filled with love as he continued to wait for me to address him. "O.K., let's see, what's a fitting name? Adam. . . I'll call him Adam. Adam, please send the energy you are holding through my system." Instantly, the spheres again zoomed past me and I felt wonderful.

"That's so cool!" I found myself exclaiming. "You mean all this time, every time I've battled fatigue, all I needed to do was ask?"

"Yep," he nodded. "Well, ask and supply and clear out the density. . . that'll do it for you 'cause the pattern you gave him to use in the first place wasn't for a body that was supposed to be tired or sick or not right somehow. For what you came here for, I think that was the right thing to do. . . you know, use a strong body pattern. Sometimes, it's better for your work on

Earth to use some other kind of pattern, or even a pattern that will make for a short lifetime, or. . ."

As usual, he seemed happy to chirp along while I had stopped, my mind caught on a piece of information like a jacket sleeve snared on a branch in the woods. "Daniel. . . you keep using this word 'pattern'. . . something I chose to use when I came here. Came from where? What are you talking about?"

Chapter 17

"I hate my body. Why can't I do something about this awful belly? God, I'm so fat. . . there's Gary, he looks great, why can't I get it together about anything, what should I do about the house payment. . . if I send it now, it will get there early and I could get the interest in the account for a few more. . . boy, I wish I was already home. I hate my body, I wish I was a little taller. . .that guy sure looks good. God, I don't like the way my business is going, I wonder if some more advertising would be useful. Did I close the garage door before I left? I'm hungry. . . can't I ever just do without food for a little while. . . no wonder I look like this. . . a sandwich sounds good and a donut. . . why are you like this? Look at that guy, he must eat the right things all the time. . . if I could just get it together. . . I wonder if the car needs to be serviced, have to remember to check when I get home. . . maybe next year, I can buy that house I saw the other day. Boy, I don't like Jack. . . he's so petty. . . so cheap. . . I don't even like the way he looks. What if we don't have enough money? What am I going to do. . . I don't like Evelyn either. She really bugs me. . . the way she criticizes everybody. . . God, I'm so fat, my pants are too tight. . . a chicken salad sandwich sounds good. . . did I set the sprinkler system?"

To my amazement, another figure had appeared out of the darkness. A small man, he was nonetheless powered by incredible, nervous energy. Moving in circles, he talked rapidly, seemingly unaware of our presence. However, Adam, the nature spirit, seemed deeply affected by this stranger as he continued with sentences which did not seem to connect with one another. "What if I can't pay my bills. . . if everyone would just do it the way I tell them to, we wouldn't be in this mess. . . I need to go past the dry cleaner and pick up my. . . won't fit, I hate this body. . . maybe a maple tree would grow in that area next to. . . I wonder if they can get the spots out of the upholstery. . . business, what can I do to bring in some more business. . .''

"Daniel," I whispered. "Who is that? Adam seems upset." Upset was not the right word. Adam was cringing as the stranger circled around him. The light that had infused him had dimmed. In fact, he seemed smaller somehow. Several spheres of energy were in his hands, but he seemed confused about what to do next. Adam began to cry, great tears falling across his cheeks. His body became bent and the spheres fell to his feet unnoticed.

Quickly grabbing a few of the balls, the stranger rasped, "Give me those!" The giant's sorrow seemed as deep as the ocean. He began to sway and I was afraid he was about to crumple to the ground.

"We've got to do something!" I said urgently. "That man's destroying Adam!"

"He's a really unfortunate creation, don't you think?" Daniel said sadly. "There's really no purpose to him at all. . . just another one of those awful misunderstandings you all have. I'll try to help, but watch what happens." With that, the little boy approached the frenetic man.

"You know, everything is perfectly all right," he said very quietly. The man did not acknowledge his existence, but continued to ramble.

Daniel persisted in trying to gain the man's attention, now moving with him as he ran in circles. "It's all right to calm down."

"I wish someone else would take some responsibility around here. . . I guess I should get the dog's teeth cleaned, they say it adds years to his life. . . I should get my own teeth cleaned. . . it's hard to read the numbers on our house, I'll have to fix that. . . the gutters. . . if I don't get them cleaned out, water isn't going to drain where it's supposed to and we could have real problems. . . I hate my body, I wonder how much Glen makes. . . I'm hungry. . . some chips would taste good."

I looked with amazement at the scene before me. Formerly luminous, the giant nature spirit had become a tragic figure, sobbing and frightened, unable to cope with the spheres of light. The insane stranger seemed to gain more energy as he talked, moving faster and faster. The little boy was caught up in trying to get his attention, so far without any success.

I jumped back involuntarily when Daniel suddenly shouted, "Stop! Just stop for a second!"

The man came to an abrupt halt, astonishment widening his eyes and stopping his speech. He took a deep breath and started moving again. "I

80

can't stop. What would happen? Who would take responsibility? Everyone else can stop, but I have so much to do. When I get everything all done, perhaps I will stop, but there's too much to do. If Brad would just do what he says he will do, I could stop, but I hate my body, I wonder if the driveway needs to be resurfaced. . . maybe a cold beer, no, that's too many calories. . . I should get those Shakespeare tickets before they sell out. . . what can I do to get some additional money coming in. . . I should have taken time to run today. . ."

"Daniel, do something!" I was desperate to help Adam. This stranger was thoroughly repulsive, oblivious to the pain he was causing. "Stop! Stop!" I found myself crying out. "Please, stop! Can't you see what you're doing to Adam?" I ran in front of the man who stopped speaking for a moment and then began again.

"I have work to do, lots of work to do. I'm responsible for so much. . . should be more time in the day. . . got to keep moving." He could barely breathe as the random words continued to flow. Trying to get around me, he seemed desperate to keep walking. I insisted on blocking his way and he looked at me with fear, like an animal trapped in someone's headlights. Suddenly, he changed. "You should feel sorry for me. After all, I have to do everything. Without my work, what would happen around here?"

"Things would go a lot better!" I blurted, feeling completely justified in my attack.

"Good! Oh, Rick, that's so good!" I was surprised to hear Daniel's enthusiasm. After all, I hadn't done anything anyone else wouldn't have done. This man was out of control. He had to be stopped before he destroyed poor Adam.

"Better. . . better, you say? Things would go out of control. . . I'm in charge of everything. Without me, there would be a horrible mess. People would find out about how much we don't know. People would discover our secrets. . . you know, all the things we don't know how to do. It's my job to make sure nobody finds out who I really am. They wouldn't like me, you know. I wonder how many calories are in one chocolate chip cookie? Do you think there are more in frozen yogurt? I really do need to get back to work. I hate my body." Off he went again, this time running in a circle eight pattern.

"Stop him, Daniel!" I didn't know what to do next. I had given it my best shot.

"You stop him, Rick!" the little boy shouted. "Come on, you can do it!"

I looked over at Daniel and cried, "I don't know how! What can we do? He's so determined!"

I was tremendously frustrated as I saw the man steal another sphere from Adam. This was an awful experience. I didn't want to be one of those people who watches someone being mugged on the street and does nothing. Adam didn't seem able to protect himself at all. I've never been able to stand the thought of someone being victimized. What one human being can do to another is astounding.

I felt a familiar surge of adrenalin shoot through my system. "All right! That's enough!" My voice surprised me. Sounding like General MacArthur commanding the troops, my tone conveyed the unequivocal message that what I said was going to happen, period, end of discussion. Moses probably sounded like that, I thought as the man stopped, looking completely confused.

"That's good!" Daniel cried out. "Rick, that's so good!" Why was this little boy always so pleased with things that were out of character for me? Every time I behaved in a way which was completely unusual for me, he was overjoyed.

I'll have to ask him about that, I thought as I continued with my WWII impression, "Stop hurting Adam! Knock it off and get the hell out of here!"

To my horror, the small man sat down and started to cry. "Damn!" I muttered. "I didn't expect him to do that. What should I do now?"

Daniel whispered his reply, "Rick, don't let him get away with that. If you let him, he'll just do the same thing in a different way. Tell him you know what he's up to!"

"But I don't!" Now I was confused. "I don't even know who he is, let alone what he's up to."

The man began another soliloquy, "Nobody understands how hard it is, I'm responsible for everything. . . I don't like how I'm treated, after all what would happen without me. . . I keep all the secrets. . . I get everything done and I work very, very hard. . . I deserve better than this. . . if they would just look at it my way, then. . ." To my astonishment, he suddenly jumped up and snatched another sphere from Adam.

"That's mine!" he snarled.

"I said stop!" The words came from somewhere deep inside myself, powered by an intensity I had seldom known. The man promptly sat down and looked balefully in my direction. "That's incredible," I muttered to Daniel. "Give him any room at all and he takes off!"

"Yep." The little boy gazed at the man who now looked like his plug had been pulled. "Look at Adam," he said softly.

Light began to course through Adam's body and began to build. Soon, he was filled with the power of a river approaching the sea. Rods of gorgeous, iridescent light shot out from his hands and a magnificent smile further illuminated his face.

"He's so beautiful!" I exclaimed. "Thank God we got that horrible person under control! How can we make sure he doesn't start up again? Who is he, anyway?"

Daniel began to giggle. "Who do you think he is, Rick?" His eyes danced as he waited for my answer.

"I don't know! How would I know? Why do you insist on expecting me to automatically understand things I have no experience with?" He could be absolutely maddening, I thought as he continued to laugh. "Come on, Daniel. Just tell me who he is."

Up went the little arms in a familiar exuberant gesture. "He's you, of course! Who else could he be?" With that, the boy disappeared.

Chapter 18

"Me!" I was astounded by Daniel's answer. And more importantly, my feelings were hurt. I wasn't like that man at all. I would never behave that way. He was so out of control. Caught up in my reaction to the little boy's unexpected insult, I did not notice my surroundings.

"Well, not really you, just what you think is you," the familiar voice said.

I looked up, expecting to see Daniel. I was standing on a magnificent black beach. Black sand, this must be Hawaii, I thought. Good. I can cope with that. I'll worry about how I got here later. "Where are you, Daniel?" I called out.

"Right here, of course." he replied, but I could see nothing but empty beach.

I loved Hawaii. Once you moved away from Waikiki, there was something so magical about the islands. For a moment, I peacefully watched the aquamarine waves greet the beach. The air here was so pure, flowers and salt water blending together in an ancient perfume. I took in a deep breath and sank my feet into the warm sand. "O.K., Daniel. Come out, wherever you are."

"I'm right here. Just like I said." Out of the corner of my eye, I saw him approaching. Wearing nothing but bright red swimming trunks, he looked like any other little kid ready for a day at the beach.

He'd better put on some sunscreen, I thought before I realized it was a ridiculous concept. This child could disappear at will. We had traveled in impossible ways to impossible places. Somehow, his white skin would survive the tropical sun without the assistance of modern chemistry. "I don't think it was very nice to say that awful man was me. I'm not anything like that!" I said, my hurt feelings coming back to the forefront. "Why did you say that? Who was he, really?"

"Like I said, he's you. . . or at least he's what you think of as you," he replied brightly.

"O.K." I said wearily. "Do we have to play another game? Why are you telling me he's me when clearly he's not?"

He looked at me very seriously, sunshine bouncing off his blond hair. "Think about it, Rick. Isn't that what you think you are? Day to day, isn't that what goes on in your mind?"

I thought for a moment as I watched the waves. "Well, there are some similarities. I do think about my responsibilities. . . I do have a business to run and I have a lot of things to take care of. . . and, I do wish I was a little thinner, but I'm not like that man."

"Yep, you are. . . that's you!" Daniel ran across the sand toward the water, little legs pumping hard. He reached the water and began to play, splashing happily, oblivious to my discomfort. "Come on, Rick. Let's play!"

"We don't have time to play," I called out irritably. "We have to get back. I have too much to do. Maybe someday, when everything's under control at work and at home. . . there are too many things to be concerned about to just waste time playing. . ."

"See!" He laughed and looked at me intently, a piece of seaweed perched perilously over one ear. "That's what you think of as you. . . stuff that goes on all the time in your mind. . . what you have to do, what you're responsible for. . . what other people think about you."

"But. . ." I replied, once again confused.

"And," he admonished, "you shouldn't keep saying you hate your body. . . that really makes Adam upset!"

"Adam! I'm the one who saved Adam! I wouldn't do anything to upset him; he doesn't deserve that!" I protested, my emotions contrasting loudly with the beautiful setting.

"You're right, Rick. He doesn't deserve that," he agreed. "You did save him. . . that was really good, but you also abuse him and that's not good at all. Keep doing that and he can't give you what you need. . . pretty soon, you get sick and worn down and then. . . well, you know what happens then."

"No, what happens then?" How was I supposed to know?

"Silly! You die, of course. . ." He ran off down the beach while I battled my anxiety. I decided to sit down for a while. If it was true that Adam was in charge of my body, it did make sense that the crazy man belonged to me as well. And, I could definitely see what kind of an impact that man had on Adam. I remembered how he had let several spheres chaotically fall to the ground. If that happened often enough, I supposed I would run out of energy. Besides that, if Adam was in charge of all my body systems, he'd better not be distracted like that.

"See, Rick. . ." I jumped as Daniel came up behind me. How did he do that? Just a moment ago, he was several hundred yards down the beach. "See, that man is what you end up with when something really wonderful gets all messed up!"

"O.K., I give up. What do you mean?" At least we weren't someplace weird, I consoled myself with that thought. Hawaii was perfectly normal. We weren't standing in mid-air, we weren't inside my body, we hadn't traveled down into a plant. This was good. Hawaii. I liked Hawaii.

"Well, like I was saying before, when you decide to come here, you send your nature spirit out to start constructing a body for you to have while you're here. You also send out another spirit. His job is to help you find the information that you're supposed to gather up. He's really cool, he just looks out peacefully and collects what you need. He gets along really well with Adam, which is good because you can see, he's really sensitive. . . so, if you can just let him do what he's. . . "

Daniel had plopped down beside me and was content to keep talking. Unfortunately, my mind had made a decision to stop like an unwilling horse in the hands of an inept rider. "Wait! Hold it! Came from where? Another spirit? How many of these spirits do I have!" I shook my head, hoping the movement would somehow arrange these pieces of information in an acceptable form.

"Three," he said simply and watched for my reaction.

"Three?" I whispered, knowing full well he was not going to retract his original statement. "Daniel, I was always taught we had one spirit."

Actually, that was not precisely true. Often, I had heard from one source or another that there was no such thing as spirit at all. Carbon-based units set to self destruct at 7.2 decades. . . that's us. I had never really believed that. But three spirits? What was he talking about?

"Yep," he nodded. "And, they're all beautiful when they're left to be what they are. But people forget so fast and then, everything gets messed up and they get all confused and the next thing you know, you've got a sick Adam, a really mean man and the other one can't even find a way to talk to you any more."

"The other one. . . " I asked weakly, quickly pleading, "please, please, please let's not go anywhere for a little while. Let's just stay here and take it nice and slow."

"O.K.," he agreed, shrugging his small shoulders. "See that mean man doesn't really mean to be mean, if you know what I mean. . ."

I'm still in the hands of an incoherent person, I thought, panic beginning to rise. What's going to happen to me? Just breathe, take in this lovely beach. Calm down. After all you've been through, it can't get much worse. Relax. Accept there's nothing you can do at this point. Breathe.

"That's good, Rick!" Daniel said happily. "Take in some good air and tell Adam to just slow everything down for you."

"Daniel. . . am I going to be all right?" I needed to hear it, even if I didn't believe it.

"Oh Rick, I sure hope so. . . " he answered, looking very worried.

"That's not very reassuring," I protested.

"Well, it's all up to you. You're the only one who can help yourself." He looked up at me with those clear, blue eyes.

"But I didn't get myself into this situation," I continued to protest. "I mean, I was riding along in an airplane and you showed up. . . next thing I know, I've lost my mind!"

"But that's the problem Rick," he said quietly. "You haven't yet lost your mind. I wish you would. See, it wasn't supposed to be there in the first place!" He finished this announcement by starting for the water.

"Wait! What do you mean? I wasn't supposed to have a mind?" I called after him. What the hell did he mean? I had to have a mind, how else could I function, think, know anything? The thought of losing it was really scary. They'll find me mumbling on a street somewhere. I won't be able to work. I'll lose my house. I won't have any control over myself.

"See, that's exactly how he does it!" Daniel shouted from the water. "That's exactly how that mean man convinces you to keep him around. But he messes everything up. . . just the opposite of what you think!"

I walked slowly toward the child. "But Daniel, how would I be without any mind? You know, 'I think, therefore I am'." My toes celebrated when they entered the water. This is heaven. . . if I'm losing my mind, at least it happened in heaven.

"You'd use your other mind. . . the one that works!" He replied matter of factly.

"My other mind?" Funny what becomes important when you're under severe stress. I suddenly became very concerned about what I was wearing. This is not appropriate at all for the beach, I ruminated, surveying my long pants and flannel shirt. I was on my way to London, looking perfectly normal. If anyone sees me out here, they're going to call the loony bin and demand an immediate pick up.

"See! He's at it again. . . worrying about what other people are going to think about you. That's how he talks you into letting him stay."

"So, you're telling me that the man who was torturing Adam is my mind. . . some kind of mind that I wasn't supposed to have and should get rid of, but I have another mind that works?" That sounded crazy. Definitely crazy. I was going to lose my license when I got back to Idaho. Crazy people are not allowed to be counselors. . . well, at least they shouldn't be allowed to be counselors. If I lost my ability to work, well, that would be a disaster. Somehow, I had to get things under control.

"There he goes again! You've got to stand up, Rick," he chastised. "Don't let him get away with that!"

"Daniel," I said wearily. "Where did this thing come from?"

"Other people," he answered. "Right from the start, when you're in a little baby body, they start creating that mean man, actually, we can call him social mind, 'cause that's what it is. Your social mind gets filled up with all kinds of judgments and opinions. They teach it to compare you to other people all the time. They tell it you don't know anything and you're just a weak nobody who can't do a thing for himself. They teach you your body is some kind of machine thing, instead of helping you to remember Adam. And, they make you totally forget where you came from and who you really are."

"You mean parents?" I didn't like what he had said. "I had really wonderful parents. They were loving and kind. They gave me everything they had."

"I know they did, Rick," he said gently. "The thing is, they didn't remember either. Their parents provided them with a social mind, too. Their social mind taught you to have one. If you had children, you would have taught them to have one, too. Isn't that sad?"

"I guess I don't understand how it should have been." I was finished pretending I knew anything at all.

"Well," he continued. "If your parents had remembered, they could have helped you to not forget right from the start. They would have known that they helped to provide you with a body, but you were someone beyond that . . . they were just supposed to protect you while your body was little. You never belonged to them and it was never their job to shape you, or mold you, or train you or do anything to you. See, they didn't mean to create the mean man, but they didn't know what else to do because they didn't remember. They thought you were empty when you got here, but you were full! You were full right from the start!"

"Full?" What did that mean?

"Yep. . . full of intelligence, not the book kind, but the kind that runs the Universe." His voice grew tender, "And love, Rick, you were so filled with love."

"That's certainly different from the way most of us see babies. . . they look so helpless." I didn't have much familiarity with babies. I did know they couldn't do very much for themselves.

"Just because they can't control their new bodies very well for awhile doesn't mean they're empty," Daniel stated. "Anyway, their nature spirit gets a lot done in a short time. . . nine months isn't much time to build all those cells and systems. By the time they get to a first birthday, they've learned a lot about how to move around!"

"Well, what do you think parents should be doing, Daniel?" This was so strange. I was playing in the water with this little boy, asking him how parents should behave. How should he know?

He looked at me and smiled, "Reminding you from the start who you really are. Telling you all about Adam and the other two spirits that make up your being . . . helping you to remember where you came from and why . . . that kind of stuff." With that, he scooped water up in his small hands and tossed it at me. Merrily giggling away, he looked so very little, and yet he had already taught me so much. Maybe we had it all backwards. Maybe the kids were supposed to teach the grownups.

Ignoring the showers of sea water sent my way I asked, "So, you're saying this 'social mind' as you call it is really almost like some kind of implant. . . it comes from outside me?"

"Yep," he answered, stopping to examine me.

I continued on, "From other people's ideas about the world. . . other people's experiences and beliefs. . . not really mine?" I didn't like how this was beginning to sound.

"Well, some of the experiences are yours, but remember how I was talking about how you only see what you already know?"

"Well, yes," I affirmed.

"So, all you do is collect experiences that agree with what other people have already given you. . . that's all you notice and that's all you know. Pretty soon, that social mind has all the power and you don't even know he's there!"

"Why is he like that? Why does he behave that way?" Maybe this was really a part of me after all. I had a sinking feeling with that uncomfortable realization.

"He's scared, that's all," Daniel said sadly.

"Scared? Scared of what?"

"Getting ended." The little boy said cryptically.

It made no sense to me. "Getting ended?"

"Yep," he nodded. "You know, if you ever start to look at him carefully, you'll decide to stop giving him energy. If you do, he'll end. . . so he gets scared a lot. Unfortunately, there's not much reason for him to feel that way, 'cause you never look anyway."

I felt accused. "How could I look if I didn't even know he was there?"

"That's true," he agreed. "I keep forgetting you don't remember anything." He shook his head, "Wow, that's so weird how that works!"

"Daniel. . . how did this happen to us? How did we get so terribly mixed up?" I was overwhelmed for a moment with the enormity of our confusion.

I thought about what he had said about comparisons. If I thought about it, my whole life was about comparisons. How did I look? How was I doing financially? Was my home nice enough? Did people like me? It was all about competition and posturing. In truth, when I felt really good, it was usually because I had compared myself to some standard and fulfilled it to my satisfaction for a change. Did I really have an obnoxious, perpetually judging and comparing mean-spirited little man inside? You bet I did.

"He steals too, you know." Daniel interrupted my extended ruminations.
"Huh?"

"He steals every chance he gets," Daniel repeated.

"What do you mean?" Oh God, it was worse than I thought. Was I stealing without knowing it? Maybe I was one of those multiple personality disorder types. You know, people that have several different personalities living inside them. I had never stolen a thing in my life, well, except for the licorice stick I availed myself of when I was six.

My mother had taken me into Hollings Pharmacy on Fairview Avenue, and standing in front of all that candy while she and Mr. Peterson discussed her prescription overhead, I had held out as long as I could. Finally, the jumble of colors had given rise to only one. Red. Red licorice screamed at me, consuming my attention and drowning out the adult words flying above me. My hand reached out without conscious consent and before I knew it, the long strand of fragrant candy had found its way to my eager lips.

Just as the flavorful sensation reached my befuddled brain, my mother had yanked my arm with the might of a maternal warrior. "Rick! Oh Rick, how could you?"

Caught, I raised my eyes to meet the horrified look of two giants. In an instant, I was caught, tried and awaited the hanging. Maybe the Lone Ranger will come, I remember thinking in my childish attempt to save myself. Now would be a good time. . . a really good time. He can appear, Silver at full gallop, and simply sweep me up with one arm and off we'd go into high adventure. I could be a hero too, rescue people and be admired. I waited for the hoofbeats and thought I heard them coming, until I realized my mother's foot was tapping the green linoleum floor in exasperation.

"Rick, what do you have to say for yourself?" She asked, words as crisp as the autumn leaves in our backyard.

I don't remember what I said. I do know I never, ever wanted to experience that particular variety of terrible feeling inside again. I never took another thing that didn't belong to me. At least I hadn't thought so until Daniel had dropped his latest bombshell.

"Yep, he does," he said sounding rather annoyed. "And, everybody else's social mind does the same thing."

"What?" Maybe I was off the hook. It wasn't just me who was stealing. Wait a minute, what was I saying?

"Yep, they all do," he continued. "See, they want as much power as they can get and so they rob Adam first, but after that, they rob anybody else they can."

"I don't understand," I replied.

His eyes were bright. "Rick, I bet you can think about times when you've been with someone and felt really drained afterwards. . . can you?"

"Sure, Daniel," I answered. "Some people are pretty challenging." I quickly thought about various people in my life. He was right. After talking with some of them, I did feel wiped out. They weren't bad people, actually most of them were pretty nice, but boy, I couldn't wait for them to leave.

"See, you get all tired out because their social mind gets in and takes energy away from Adam," he said.

I was shocked at this latest piece of information. "What!"

"Yep, that's what happens," he said sadly. "You think it's just talking, words going back and forth, but meanwhile, their social mind comes right in and steals from Adam and you feel bad. Everybody else's social mind is scared about being ended, just like yours is."

"But Daniel. . . that's terrible!" I felt violated by these invisible robberies. "How can that be?"

"Well," he said softly, "all the social minds are pretty much out of control. They do what they want. They even talk to each other and then, it can get really confusing for people."

"Talk to each other?" I asked.

"Yep. While you are talking away and the other person is too, your two social minds talk to each other. Sometimes what they say doesn't agree at all with your out loud words. Did you ever just not like somebody and you can't figure out why?"

"Well, yes." Actually, that happened frequently. I liked to think of myself as an agreeable, accepting kind of person, but there were lots of people I really didn't like without a good reason.

He continued with his instruction, "That's because the two social minds have said stuff to each other that's not nice at all. They can even be attacking each other and trying to steal energy while you're having a regular conversation."

I stopped for a moment. There were those interactions that seemed to go wrong for absolutely no reason at all. Two nice people just at subtle odds with each other. . . sometimes not so subtle odds.

Daniel looked at me intently, "Yep, just two social minds struggling away and you never know it!" Off he skipped down the beach.

"Wait, Daniel. This is awful. No wonder people have such a hard time getting along! We don't even know what we're saying to each other. . . doesn't that get people killed sometimes? I mean, if I'm asking for directions and somehow telling the other guy his mother has an unsavory night job, well, no wonder! And wars, Daniel, how can we get to world peace with these idiots talking away without our knowledge? How do we stop them?"

"By being like those guys." Daniel stopped and pointed up the beach. I had left my glasses on the airplane. What looked like two brown paper bags seemed to be approaching.

"Them? You mean there are people in Hawaii who don't have social minds?" I was shocked. I thought he had said all human beings were basically in the same mess as me. Great! At least somebody has it right. "How did they escape, Daniel?"

"They didn't," he said quietly. "They aren't here any more."

"What? They're right there. I can see them now."

The two men had become more clear. Brown and muscular, they headed straight toward us. They smiled and there was something different about them. They seemed radiant, that was it. That's what living in paradise can do for you, I thought. They looked so healthy, actually, they were quite beautiful.

"What do you mean, they aren't here any more?"

"Well, they're here, but not there," Daniel said, grinning up at the new arrivals.

There was something odd about these two guys, but I couldn't put my finger on it. They were so full. That was it. They didn't seem to need anything at all. That was an interesting revelation as I thought about it. Most people need something from you. Now, I could understand a little better; most people had a social mind that needed energy. When I talked to anyone, that out of control, awful little man inside them was invisibly plotting about how to get more energy for himself. The bottom line was, everybody I talked to needed energy. But, these two didn't.

What a different feeling it was to be near them. Somehow, they were giving to me. . . I could feel it. . . their presence was making me feel better, stronger, more safe. As I looked at them in amazement, I was aware of something rising from my feet, through my legs, traveling through my lower body, up into my chest, warm, nurturing, fulfilling, peaceful.

"God! How do you do that?" I whispered, feeling incomprehensibly grateful. It suddenly dawned on me, what I was feeling was love, some kind of love in a tangible form. They were offering love and somehow I could feel its energy. This wasn't conceptual love. . . "we should all love one another" stuff. This was literally an offering of energy, freely given, mine to have, no strings attached.

"Thank you." I breathed, my eyes wide as my body continued to fill with the wonderful energy.

"See, that's what Jesus meant when he said to love each other," Daniel said brightly. "He meant give each other actual energies of love, not ideas about love. You just have to do what they're doing and things could be a whole lot better!"

I was bursting with the delicious feeling. "Why did you say they weren't here. They certainly are!"

"Well, they're here, but not there," he said, making no sense at all.

"Huh?"

"Well, just look!" There were those words again. But I was now eager to look. Whatever I had to see to explain the wonderful experience I had just had with these two strangers, I wanted to see. But nothing could possibly prepare me for what happened next.

Chapter 19

The sky had gone softly gray and the sea the color of spent charcoal. I was calm inside, filled up with the energies of love given to me by the two mysterious men on the beach. But, they seemed long gone now as the warm wind brushed my face. The little child stood by my side and I searched the horizon for something; what I did not know.

"See!" His voice was joyful. I did not see anything but a beautiful silver band far out across the water. The shimmering light broke the line of gray extending from sea to sky. I watched the gulls fly effortlessly in front of us and then returned my attention to the strip of light across the horizon.

"See!" he repeated.

I was so peaceful inside. Why had I never known this feeling before? For once, there was nowhere to go and nothing to do. I wasn't trying to get anything or come up with anything. I knew I could not and need not impress Daniel.

We stood together, unencumbered, simple, beautiful as the shore itself. The silver band grew wider and even more luminous. It seemed somehow to be moving toward us and I thought about how magnificent Hawaii can be. Mesmerized now, caught in the warm breeze, the sensation of being completely full, I watched the light as it slowly moved. This is a very strange atmospheric condition of some kind. The thought was almost jarring. . . social mind trying to compartmentalize.

"That's so good, Rick!" Daniel rewarded me with a shower of enthusiasm. I was actually pleased with myself. I had recognized the intruder and stopped him in his tracks. My reward, a continuation of this blissful state of being. "Just watch," he reminded me gently.

Indeed, there was something most compelling to watch. The gray sky moved back farther and farther as the band of light widened and approached the shore. The gulls in front of us suddenly stopped moving. Mid-flight, they simply ceased and suspended in the air, they too seemed caught in some kind of magic. "Daniel, what's going on here?"

I had slipped just a little bit with the aerodynamically impossible accomplishment of the birds. And then I noticed the waves had stopped. Half crested, the white spray on top of the swelling waves was suspended as well, droplets of water staying just where they were without any movement at all.

I looked quickly over at the small boy at my side to see his face radiant with joy. Light streamed from every pore of his little body. I turned my head to see the band had almost reached us. If we did not move, we would shortly be caught in it completely. I did not know what that meant, I only knew I did not want to run.

Daniel spoke so softly, his words floated in the wind like the gull feathers drifting across the sand. "Just stay right here, Rick. . . not only with your body. . . but stay where you are right now in your heart."

How beautiful this place was, everything so delicately balanced, so rhythmically associated, each thing having its perfect place. And I was a part of it all. I had my place as well. For once, I was not an anxious consumer on the surface of the environment. . . I had an integral part, as important, but not more important than anything or anyone else here. And the sound, suddenly I became aware of the sound. A low humming rose up around us; it seemed to be coming tenderly from everywhere. I looked down to find each grain of sand with its own voice. Like a gigantic choir surrounding us, everything sang the same song. Tears swept down my face and I found myself sobbing for everything I had not known.

"Daniel, it's all alive, isn't it? My God, it's all alive! I never knew. . . why did I not know all this time it's all been alive?" And even as I cried, I was still full of love. My tears acted to clear away the debris in my heart and mind. And it all began to move. In one majestic, integrated, harmonious swaying motion, it all began to move.

My body joined without conscious volition and for a few glorious seconds we all sang one song and danced one dance together. And my arms grew feathers and became wings and my feet became hoofed and galloped across the beach and my hands turned in perfect spirals and nautilus shells grew. All at once, I became everything that could be and still the silver band continued its journey toward us.

"See, that's what happens when you're in your right mind. . . isn't it beautiful?" Everything spoke at once, the words not coming only from Daniel this time. Simultaneously, I had said the same thing! Somehow, I knew to say the same thing. More important, somehow I knew the same thing. How? Where did that come from?

Again, we all spoke at once, "That's your right mind. . . the mind you were meant to have, the one that's gotten covered over by the implanted social mind. You see, the right mind can see the whole, it doesn't separate and judge, it just watches everything in love."

We continued, "When you're in your right mind, there is no competition for energy, for you have all you need. When nothing is separated, there is no lack. When you are not falsely isolated, there is no need to fear or worry, for you have absolutely everything all at once."

"You mean, this is the way I could feel all the time?" I whispered, this time speaking all alone.

"Of course," we all replied. "This is how you were meant to feel and be while you are on the Earth."

Looking down, I found myself now clearly in my own body again. But, somehow illuminated from within, I appeared like a paper lantern, soft light showing through my skin. Daniel stood at my side, entranced by the profoundly beautiful ribbon of silver light, now just off shore. Almost filling the sky, I could see shimmering particles of light moving within the band. Unsure, I thought I saw shapes beginning to form almost out of the light itself. Faces and bodies softly emerged and disappeared again.

"Is there anyone in there, Daniel?"

"See!" he replied enthusiastically. I looked with renewed concentration inside the ribbon of light. As if out of an incandescent fog, people began to move outwards and toward us. They were beautiful, just like the men on the beach. . . strong, muscular, brown and joyful. I was not afraid, but I was confused.

"Daniel, is that some sort of space craft?" I ventured. "Is that what this is all about. . . are they visitors from another planet, come to save us?"

Once again I heard rippling laughter, sent out with love not judgment. "Oh Rick. . . Rick, is it so hard to accept who you are?"

I sputtered, "But, I am not like them. . . am I, Daniel? I mean, I don't seem to be. . . at least not until the last few minutes or so. What is that light? Where are they coming from? Who are they, anyway?" I continued to babble as I watched streams of joy in the form of human beings emerge out of the band.

"They're people, silly!" he laughed. "They're Earth people! They're Earth people who are in their right minds! Isn't that a funny phrase? You guys use it all the time, except you don't know what you mean when you say, 'he's not in his right mind.' See?"

"I'm sorry. I don't understand," I whispered. "They are so beautiful, Daniel, their bodies are transparent somehow, I mean, I can see light shining through them from somewhere inside."

"Yep. You, too." he pointed out. Sure enough, my body continued to radiate light.

I tried to make sense out of what he was saying. "How can you say they are Earth people? I saw them come out of that light. I saw that band move all the way from the horizon to here. I've never seen anything like that before, not even in Hawaii!"

"But, we're not in Hawaii. . ." he stated quietly.

"We're not in Hawaii?" I decided to sit down as these gorgeous beacons of light formed a circle of loving energy around me.

Struggling to keep my social mind at bay, I was aware it had set up an enormous protest within me. I knew it had started attacking Adam for energy. The argument was so familiar by now, "Get it together, Rick. It's time to stop all this nonsense and get concerned, worried, downright afraid. After all, look at what's happened to you today. Do you consider that normal? You've gone crazy, that's what it is and you need help. Just let me take care of you, Rick. Let's get away from this kid and all the other hallucinations and see if we can contact reality again. After all, you have a practice to run, bills to pay, obligations to meet. What are people going to think? You can't afford to go crazy. . . "

"No!" I shouted at full volume. "No! You can't rob me any more. You can't take my life away from me any more. I deserve to know who I am!"

Waves of joy swept over me as the energy of those surrounding me seemed to arc up even higher. Daniel beamed and patted my arm, "That's good, Rick. That's so good."

I felt incredibly strong in that moment. Every aspect of my being seemed to vibrate in recognition of my statement of liberation. I felt alive! I was filled with new courage and I was ready to find out what I needed to know. "All right. We're not in Hawaii. Fine. Where are we?"

His face was merry as he replied, "In the Earth people's first home, silly. Where else could we be?"

Chapter 20

"Could you repeat that?" I said quietly. Actually, I had heard his words just fine, but I needed time to assimilate them.

Earth people's first home, what could that mean? Hadn't we always lived on this planet? I had heard rumors from some New Age types that we had actually come from Venus, at least I think it was Venus. But that had struck me as absurd. Why was it more probable that life had started on Venus?

"No, Rick," said the little boy, once again reading my mind. "I don't mean you came from another planet. Well, at least not exactly. Well, I mean most of you didn't. Anyway, what I meant was, this is the first place on Earth where people lived. You know, after Gaia built her body to help you. . . you all came to live on this part of her body."

Gaia's body. . . Earth was not a giant, dead piece of rock, but a being who had created a body that we were currently living on. My "dream experience" with the beautiful woman had been real! Gaia! I had to accept it. The experience I had on the beach, that was real, too. Everything was alive. . . that was quite obvious. It was all alive with Gaia, because she was a sentient being with a living body.

I wanted him to confirm what I already knew. "Daniel, it's really true, isn't it? Gaia is a living person, being, whatever and human beings are supported by her. . . just like a mother supports her babies!"

"Yep. Except babies usually treat their mother a lot better than humans treat Gaia. . . " he trailed off, momentarily sounding sad.

"So," I said, excited to know this part of my history, "this is the part of Gaia where we first. . . first landed, emerged, developed, what?"

He nodded his reply as I thought to ask an obvious question, "And where are we, by the way?"

"In the Pacific," he answered.

"I thought you said we weren't in Hawaii."

"Well, we kind of are, sort of, but. . ."

"Not exactly," I finished. "Tell me please. . . where are we?"

"See, Hawaii and some other islands are what's left in your time of what's here now." He had regained his sunny disposition, but my poor social mind had caught on a single pair of words.

"My time?" I said quietly.

"Well sure," he laughed. "You didn't think we were still in the 20th century, did you? That's pretty silly. I told you that they. . . "

"Where. . . are...we?" I spoke very slowly, hoping this maneuver might help disengage the frantic grip the claws of my social mind had on the ceiling of my brain.

"Well, let's see," he mused. "Hummm. . . how would you describe it? Can't really tell you in terms of centuries like you usually do because. . ."

The need to know grew larger than my patience, "Daniel, for God's sake, spit it out!"

"About 720,000 years before your time." He replied, somewhat surprised by the degree of tension behind my words.

"720,000 years?" I said, surprise draining my impatience. "Did you say we are 720,000 years from where I usually live?" I couldn't remember my geology classes. . . were there dinosaurs in this time?

"Of course there aren't!" Daniel said instantly. "They were much earlier."

"Why did you say Hawaii is what's left?" I asked, looking around us. "Are we on another island somewhere around Hawaii?"

"Well. . . well, you could say that. It's a little bigger, well maybe a lot bigger. Let's see, I'll measure it for you." There was a long pause while Daniel's eyes gazed off in the distance. "It's 3,143 miles by 7,302 miles. That's pretty big!"

"How on Earth did you measure it!" I cried. "Are you telling me we're on a continent in the Pacific? A continent that's enormous. . . a continent that Hawaii is now a remnant of?"

"Yep," he said simply.

"Daniel, is this Atlantis?"

"Nope. They're just a colony."

"What did you say?" Asking people to repeat themselves is a really good way to buy enough time for your brain to catch up. I had heard him perfectly well the first time.

"Atlantis. . . that's in the Atlantic Ocean, silly. This is the Pacific." My dazed expression encouraged him to add more, "But lots of Earth people go from here to there and to other places on Gaia as well. But, you all started out right here. Didn't you ever wonder why you can find the same symbols all over the world? Didn't you ever wonder about how you can find the same so-called myths all over, even when the surface cultures seem really different?"

Mentally, I found a more comfortable place to stand, "Well, I read some of Carl Jung's books. . . I guess you can't know who he is, Daniel. You're way too small to have waded through Jung."

What a ridiculous statement, I thought, as soon as the words made their way out of my mouth. He may look small, but that has nothing to do with who he is!

"Well, Jung sure made an easy thing awfully complicated," Daniel said, ignoring my stupid remark. "He came up with this big mysterious theory about how all people share a single mind somehow and that's why they think up the same symbols. But you know what? You really do that because you all came from the same place. The same symbols all over the Earth isn't any different than Dutch people everywhere thinking about tulips and windmills. . . it's just part of where they came from."

I asked softly, "What do you call this place, Daniel?"

He smiled, "The people who live here don't have a name for it. . . they only have right minds, remember? No need to categorize things and separate them out."

"Are all the people on this continent like these people?" I asked looking out over the luminous group still surrounding me.

"Yep," he answered, visibly pleased with those around us. "They didn't start out that way. Boy, when you guys first got here, you were a real mess. But they came along really well. Gaia helped them and they grew great. . . not like your Earth people now."

"What do you mean?" I asked, bravely willing to have some more of my intellectual debris swept away for good.

"Well, density. . . remember when we were talking about that?" He asked, waiting for me to nod before continuing.

"Where you came from had gotten to be thick with awful density. That's why Gaia had to volunteer. . . to get you out of there. Well, these guys took good advantage of their opportunity to drop the density and be on their way back home, but you guys. . . well, you guys just keep getting heavier and heavier. . . that's why Gaia is having such a terribly hard time. She was never made to carry the kind of weight you guys keep piling on."

"Daniel, that's so horrible," I cried. "We are brutally damaging a living being! And, it's the being who takes care of us. What's the matter with us?"

"You're lost," he replied looking deeply concerned. "You're all just awfully lost."

"You keep referring to us coming from somewhere else. . . where?" Seeing a slight hesitation I added, "Didn't you just say we didn't come from another planet?"

"Yep," he confirmed. "Well, some of you came from other planets, but not the ones in your solar system. . . but most of you have only had bodies on Gaia."

Some of the people on Earth came from other planets. I silently decided I would ask about that later. Right now, I was much more interested in where I had come from, more accurately, where the earlier people on Earth had come from. "So, what do you mean when you talk about how these people were when they first got here? Where were they in the first place?"

"Let's eat!" The little boy sprang suddenly to his feet and running off into the thick green underbrush, he disappeared from sight. I looked around to find only deep, compassionate eyes gazing at me from all directions. One man reached out his hand and I clasped it tightly, and was instantly infused with love. I did not know where I was, but I wanted to stay here forever.

A large, bright yellow fruit was offered from someone else, and I gladly took it. Savoring the delicious, unfamiliar taste, I was for the first time aware that it was a gift directly to me from Gaia. I stopped eating and closed my eyes for a moment. "Thank you, dear Gaia. Thank you for your gifts to me, for so long taken without gratitude. Thank you for never giving up. . . for standing firm underneath my feet, for allowing me to breathe and eat. Thank you for the clear water you send from the sky which sustains me and washes me clean. Thank you for volunteering to care for me. . ."

I felt deeply moved in that moment, realizing I had to thank this being for my very life. How do you do that? How do you thank someone who has given you life for forty three years without ever being thanked even once?

I thought about how heartless human beings had been all this time, carving great wounds across her body, burning down her forests, paving over her skin, making it impossible for her to breathe in the fumes from our miserable machines.

"I am so sorry. . ." I whispered, hoping my words would find their way directly into her heart. "I apologize for all of us. . . I am so sorry." With that, I fell into her arms and knowing I was indeed a child of the Earth, allowed myself to sleep.

Chapter 21

"Hi." I heard a small voice somewhere off to my left. I had slept, but for how long?

"Hi." The little voice came again. I made what seemed like a monumental decision to open one eye. It was dark and I was still on the beach; the waves were moving again. I could hear them breaking against the shore. Sitting up, I looked around and saw no one.

"Hi." This didn't sound like Daniel.

"I can't see you, whoever you are," I replied.

"Down here. Look down here." Attempting to locate the voice, I searched downward, but saw only obsidian sand in the black night.

"You have to use your abilities." Again, the apparently disembodied voice spoke. "That's the only way to see anything real."

"I don't have any abilities," I said sadly. "I'm beginning to realize that. My social mind, do you know what that is, whoever you are?"

"I know what it is," came the reply.

"Well, my social mind kept me from realizing I even had anything except it. I didn't even know I had Adam, let alone abilities of any kind. I still don't know what they might be or how to use them. I'm not even sure who I am any more." I had no idea who I was talking to, but somehow it felt safe. "Daniel, is that you?"

"No."

Hoping for further information, I waited in the silence for a moment before asking, "Who are you?"

"Use your abilities." Sounding encouraging, the voice continued, "You do have them, even when you don't realize that you do. All of Earth's people have them. That's the point, really."

"I don't know how," I answered, feeling a little sorry for myself. "I don't even know what they are."

I heard a gentle reply, "Where would you start to look?"

"I have no idea," I said without thinking.

"Sure you do, Rick," the voice answered tenderly. "What have you been feeling since you've been here?"

That question was easy to answer, "A tremendous amount of love. . . some kind of tangible energy that these people just seem to give away to each other and to me."

"Right." The voice sounded pleased. "And where do you feel that love the most?"

"Well, all over my body. . ." That wasn't quite right. "In my heart the most."

"So. . ." it prompted in the darkness.

Excitedly I replied, "So, look for my abilities in my heart!"

"That's right!" Softly it encouraged me again, "Just like I said, look down."

Hoping I had understood what the voice meant, I glanced down to my chest. Astonished, I found a light in the darkness. Pulling the shirt away from my skin, I saw beyond the surface and straight into the center of my chest. But what was there was not an anatomical structure at all. Instead, turning slowly was some kind of beautiful, compelling light, organized into a ball. My heart seemed to be divided into sections, turned slowly by flexible membranes of light, slightly billowing, like sails in a gentle wind.

"What is that?" Filled with peace, I was not afraid to hear the answer.

There was no need to fear anything I might learn on this incredible flight through the unknown. My God, it was beginning to appear that human beings had been tricked, led into a series of beliefs about who we are which only made us more and more lost. I wanted to know. I wanted what was mine to begin with.

"That's you," the voice responded. "That's the part of you that receives the energy from your soul and propels it throughout your being so you can live on Earth. That's your central point while on Earth. . . the place where all the love comes in to sustain you while you are here. And, if you are willing to listen, that's where you can best hear the voice of your soul."

"It's so beautiful." I could hardly believe something like this belonged to me. How could I deserve something so incredibly beautiful?

"Rick, you don't have to deserve it," the voice replied. "It is you. It isn't something given as a reward for being good or accomplished in some way. It is you. . . that's what we have been trying to tell you. Pure love exists at the center of your being. And, it is meant to flow freely throughout your entire being, but. . ."

I knew what was coming next and interrupted, "I get it! I get it! Density! Density is what gets it all clogged up, right? And that social mind thing we all end up with. That just grabs all the energy and diverts it into judgments and segmenting and separating and developing opinions and all that stuff! We're supposed to be like the people here. . . just the energy of love running clear and smooth through our system and out to one another. That's it! That's it, isn't it!"

"That's so good!" Daniel had appeared out of the darkness. "Rick, that's so good!"

"Look, Daniel! Look at my heart!" I excitedly pointed to the beautiful ball still softly turning.

"I know. . . that's what I see in everybody all the time," he said smiling. "You're all like that, you just forget when you get here and then it takes you forever to remember and then. . ."

"Daniel," I had an important question. "Who was talking to me?"

"You'll meet them a little later," he replied. "Right now, we have somewhere we need to go."

"Can I take this with me?" I said, concerned I might lose this newly discovered wonder within me.

Daniel looked up at me with amusement and I answered my own question, "Oh. Right. It is me. That's right. This is me! I can't leave it anywhere, can I?" I felt incredibly empowered. I was not that nasty, stealing, little man, after all. I had this wondrous energy inside. . . that was me.

"Of course you can't lose it someplace, silly," he affirmed. "Let's go. I want you to see something."

Dawn was beginning to break, gorgeous, delicate colors of pink and lavender pushing back the darkness. The scent of salt water and flowers wafted by on the warm breeze. As I walked behind the little boy skipping in the early morning light, I knew I would follow him anywhere. Passion was finding its way to the surface from somewhere deep within me. I was filled with courage and a new kind of strength that seemed to be coming straight from my light-filled heart.

I had a right to know what had been hidden from me, from all of us. I wanted permanent freedom from that social mind. I wanted to take care of Adam. And, I wanted to know about this soul that spoke to me. I had never heard it. Had it been talking to me all the time?

"Yep," Daniel called over his bare little shoulder. "Yep. It talks all the time."

"Daniel, am I ever going to be able to do that? You know, read other people's minds?" His capacity was still quite unnerving to me.

"Sure," he said simply. "But, it's mostly just social mind chattering and blaming and pushing and stealing kinds of stuff. It's way better when you start listening to a person's heart. . . that's a completely different thing."

"I can imagine." I thought about the nonsense my own social mind had thrown my way. Compared to the peaceful, loving energy that came from my heart, it was tragic to think about the loss of time humanity had suffered frantically running back and forth, chasing our neurotic fears and concerns all over the landscape.

We tried so hard to find peace and love for ourselves. "Looking for love in all the wrong places." That was a country song, I thought. So accurate, but yet the way they meant it, so terribly wrong. Love wasn't somewhere outside in the form of another lost human being who was as cut off and desperate as you were. And peace. . . that couldn't come from finally getting all your bills paid and your worries settled. . . and peace sure didn't show up at the bottom of a bottle or container of pills. "Better living through biochemistry" could only take us so far. Sure, it could help to get some people through their days, but it didn't really lead anywhere. There had to be more to life than that. . . everyone knew it somewhere inside. We were all just afraid to say anything because we didn't have the slightest idea about what it might be.

I wanted more, "Daniel, this soul. . . my soul talks to me all the time?"

"Yep," he said, continuing to walk down the beach.

"What does it say?" I knew his answer was not going to be simple.

He was not ready to tell me. "I think you should hear that for yourself."

"But, I always thought the soul was somewhere else. . . I don't know, like in heaven or something. That seems very far away."

"Nope." The sky was considerably brighter now and the sea had turned a clear blue, like Daniel's eyes. "That's just more misunderstanding. Your soul isn't far away at all. . . see, you're actually in the middle of it. Really, you have to work pretty hard not to hear it."

"In the middle of it?" What in the world did that mean?

"Yep. See, even when people know they have a soul, they've been trained to think it's really far away or that it's some kind of tiny spark in them, but that's not right at all."

He was right about that. When I had considered my soul, it had always seemed very distant. . . foreign somehow. . . something to consider later. "Well Daniel, what's right. . . what do you mean I'm in the middle?"

"Well. . . well. . . well, just look!"

Chapter 22

I did not know where I was, but it did not matter at all. Spectacular beauty surrounded me, and love. . . love was everywhere; this place seemed constructed of love itself. Sheets of pure, incandescent light undulated across an endless plane and for all those miles there was nothing but love. My heart was as full as the sea and my mind. . . my mind was gone.

Somehow, even the concept of wondering where I was seemed uncommonly strange. "Where" was irrelevant for without a mind, I was suddenly no one and everyone and this was somewhere and nowhere. And I was so full. . . oh God, I had struggled so hard and so long to feel this way. My worries had gone with my mind, like the garbage goes with the trash bag.

And my heart. . . my heart turned and radiated the most wondrous light. It sent rays out in every direction and light flowed through my body unchallenged and unstoppable. Unconditionally, bountiful light and love poured from a limitless source. And once received, I could send it out for miles and miles. . . I could send it to every human being in the world and I would have enough, I would have more than enough to feed every living thing forever and ever.

And Gaia, dear beautiful woman, my love, my friend, my mother, my sister, I can give to you as well. I have enough to heal you; I can wash your wounds and erase your scars. I can hold your heart in my hands and calm it again. And trees and animals will spring forth whole again. And your oceans will become clean and clear and the air. . . I can sweep the air with all this love and all of your dear ones can breathe again. Come to me, sweet Gaia. . . let me hold you up, let me soothe you and stroke you, love you and care for you and all your children. I have more than enough.

"See." Daniel's eyes found mine. "See. . . that's who you are."

Abruptly I flew backwards at an amazing speed and found myself on the beach again. Daniel held my hands in his and I was overflowing with intense gratitude.

"My soul. . . that was my soul, wasn't it?" My voice was barely audible.

The same love I had just experienced now filled his words. "Yes, Rick. That is who you are. Your body exists in the midst of that vast field of energy. It's the body and mind which are tiny, not the soul. . . that has never been small, no matter what your keepers have told you."

Tears swept down my cheeks and I whispered, "That soul. . . that soul speaks to me constantly?" Seeing his nod, I continued, "And that soul pours energy into my heart?"

"Constantly," he affirmed, gently wiping away my tears with his little hand.

"Daniel. . . what does it say? What does my soul want me to hear?" But he did not need to answer my question, for I was already hearing the voice in my heart.

"Rick, you are loved by everything that is and can ever be. You are never alone, for I am with you always. Just let go, allow me in. I cannot force my way in, nor would I ever wish to. But know, in exact proportion to the room you make, I will flow into every tiny space within you. I will fill you with anything you could ever need. Let go of the social mind, let go of your preoccupation with what it tells you. . . just let it go, Rick. Everything is perfectly all right. There is no danger except that which you bring to yourself through density. You see, density serves only to separate us, and without me, you are isolated and cannot find what you need to sustain you. Let go of all that blocks me out. Come to me, Rick. Let go. . . let me flow in. . . and through you, let me flow out into your world."

My heart blazed with a radiance rivaled only by the sun, and yet my eyes did not hurt as I watched it. Glorious, pure light moved out from me in every direction. "Daniel. . . do you mean we've had it all backwards? It's not that the soul is way out there somewhere and we have to struggle to get to it. It's been right here all along and it wants to come into us more and more, but we don't let it because we're all clogged up with density and social mind?" Overcome with gratitude, I stopped for a moment.

Gathering myself together, I continued, "It's been there the whole time! I didn't know it was up to me to make room! I was always mad because the soul didn't just show up and do something to make my life better. And prayers. . . all this time, my soul couldn't answer because I wasn't letting it come in! I thought it didn't work because prayers were useless sentimentality."

The realization that humanity had been so lost for so long was tremendously sad. It was so clear to me now. We had been berating the cosmos for not saving us from our difficulties in life. We had been fearing some vengeful God out there, thinking we weren't good enough to be cared for. And all the time, our soul was right here! We were right in the midst of all of that love which was just waiting for us to make a little bit of room so it could flow in. And that powerful, punishing God. . . it was just our own construction, something our social mind had created with energy stolen from Adam!

The child watched me grapple with the reality of our confusion for a minute then stated, "You've gotten awfully mixed up. See, it's up to you to clear up your density by making choices in every moment that get rid of it. That's what I've been trying to tell you. This isn't about ideas, it's about energy!"

Excitement was building within me, "We haven't been abandoned at all! Spirit isn't any farther away than it's ever been, we're just getting more and more difficult to communicate with!"

Eyes full of compassion, Daniel replied, "If you build up a thick social mind and clog up your body and your heart with density, how's your soul going to come in? It can't just blow out all your junk like the man who comes in the fall to blow out your sprinkler system! That wouldn't be right, 'cause you always have to have free will. That's the way it is on Earth."

All of this made so much sense to me. We were trying so hard to get help from something beyond ourselves, but it never seemed to work very well. From my Christian friends who constantly prayed for divine intervention, to those who looked to angels and crystals, we desperately wanted help to get us out of the personal and cultural mess we were in. But Daniel was saying that without a real effort on our part to clear away the density within ourselves, without taking personal responsibility to do the work that was required, the limitless love and help which surrounded us couldn't find room to get in!

We really didn't need to do the supplicating, the sacrificing, the candle lighting, the religious rituals, the pleading. . . the problem had absolutely nothing to do with persuading spiritual help that we were worthy of its attention. It was right there, always had been. The implications were so enormous, I decided to check out my conclusions with my young teacher. "So, all of this pleading for outside help. . . God, angels and all of that, it doesn't fix anything, does it?"

"Nope," he said sadly. "As long as people continue to keep the density they have, and probably accumulate even more, there's no room for the soul to flow in."

We had been so far off track! The voice of the infinite wasn't ever going to boom down from the sky, or even appear as a choir of angels. It was much, much closer than that. I considered for a moment how close the answers had really been the whole time. But, the last place humanity would ever look to find the soul was in its own heart.

"Daniel," I cried. "It's through my heart that I can receive the energies of love of my soul, even hear what it has to say to me, but all this time, I didn't even realize what my heart really was, let alone know to listen to it!"

"I know," he said quietly. "For some reason, Earth people worship that social mind. . . and that's about the worst thing they can do." Abruptly he leaped to his feet and marching off down the beach called out, "Let's go!"

Surprised, I watched the little boy travel across the sand for a moment before jumping up to follow him. "Where are we going? Daniel, where are we going?"

Glancing over at me, he replied, "I want you to see something really important. . . then you'll understand better, I think."

"Where, though?" I scrambled to keep up with him, "Where are we going?"

He smiled and said, "I want you to see where human beings came from in the first place." With that, he made a sharp left turn and headed toward the lush, emerald green vegetation which marked the edge of the beach. Within seconds, he had somehow reached a thick cluster of palm trees and, well ahead of me, vanished among them.

Chapter 23

All around me, rough, gray, slightly hairy trunks pointed straight to the sky like a herd of elephants flat on their backs. I rubbed the surface of the palm tree in front of me and wondered where Daniel had gone. Remembering what my soul had said about never being alone, I decided I would be all right for a while without my little guide. I was constantly surrounded by love; I knew that now.

Walking peacefully among the trees, I thought about Gaia and the multitude of animals and plants she had created. Daniel had said once that she came from heaven. I wondered what that meant. If our soul didn't live in a far off heaven somewhere, then what was heaven about? Why did Gaia come from there?

I could still hear the waves touching the beach, but it was good to be up off the sand. Here, the air was fragrant with life and I remembered what it had been like to be inside the fern. Aware of so much more than I had ever been before, I saw a thousand little green things pulling sparkling light into themselves, each one reaching independently up toward the food of its being. It seemed they knew more than we did.

How did we get so hopelessly lost? Certain things seemed so obvious to me now. Gaia was the ground of our being, the source of our bodies, or vehicles as Daniel insisted on calling them. But, the light of our soul, that was what truly created and sustained us.

These green creatures all knew to turn their faces to the sun, to stay in contact with that light to the absolute best of their ability. They knew somehow not to cover themselves up with anything that could prevent that light from entering in, for without it, they would die away.

"That social mind really isn't very smart, you know." A voice seemed to come from somewhere at my feet.

Looking down, I quickly asked, "Are you the one who was talking to me in the night?"

Not waiting for the answer I already knew, I went on, "You're the one I couldn't see! Come out this time. Please come out!" The ground under my feet was moist and the color of cinnamon; I knew it was volcanic soil, incredibly rich and fertile. Turning around to see if there was someone behind me, I saw nothing but a diverse collection of healthy plants.

"Down here." Again, I looked down at my feet and saw nothing unusual.

"Use your abilities. You can't see anything that's important if you just use your senses. . ."

I pondered the statement for a moment. "I'm supposed to go to my heart, aren't I? You told me that before! Thank you so much, whoever you are."

Receiving no answer, I concentrated on my heart, knowing about its capacity to radiate the light coming from my soul. After a moment, I looked down. . . sure enough, the shimmering glow was there. As I thought about the intense love I had recently experienced, the ball of light began to turn and grow brighter. I filled up once again with peace and wonderful energy.

"Now look."

From my blissful state of being, I looked down again and there at my feet was something I never in my wildest dreams thought I would see. "What! What in the world. . ."

"Hi," she said. At least it seemed like a she. Struggling to understand what I was seeing, I moved away from my heart and I immediately couldn't see her any more.

"Use your abilities." I renewed my concentration and there it was again.

"Hi." A small light fluttered around my right foot. Slightly larger than a butterfly, it generated a subtle array of beautiful pale colors. Now violet, then pink, peach and gentle yellow, the light never stopped moving.

"What are you. . . who are you?" I fought to keep myself securely anchored in my heart. I could feel my social mind aroused and ready to steal energy. After all, this was suspiciously close to being like a fairy of some kind. Fairies were a myth, everybody knew that, a nice legend. With that thought, the light promptly disappeared.

"Use your abilities."

"I know, I know," I said with frustration. "My social mind is so devious. If I lose my concentration for a second, bam! He's right there, ready to take over. Let me try again."

I thought about all the wondrous love I had been given and knew I did not want to take residence in social mind ever again. But that was not going to be easy. I had lived a lot of years letting him get away with everything. From now on, life was going to be different; there was too much to lose.

When I was ready, I looked down again and there she was! Enormously pleased with myself, I searched the patch of light for gossamer wings. Why not? After everything I had learned, why not accept this as well? Nonchalantly I stated, "You're a fairy, right?"

"No," she replied.

"No?" I had readied myself to accept something I thought was impossible, but it wasn't correct after all. So much for that theory. "What are you then?"

"A human being, just like you are," she said simply.

"What!" As quickly as I said it, I knew I was going to lose sight of the dazzling little light. I knew who had control of my energy in this important moment. But this time, I was not going to let him get away with it.

"Get out of my way!" I commanded social mind. And, there she was again, now like an iridescent dragonfly, oscillating by my left elbow.

"Well, not just like you are, but still. . . a human being," she said sweetly.

"But you don't seem to have a body!" I protested. "I mean, you look like pure energy. . . no form, no vehicle, as Daniel would call it. And, you're so small! You don't seem anything like a human being to me."

I tried very, very hard to keep my heart completely open while I asked my questions. I knew the best thing I could do was simply accept what I was seeing without question. . . but I was so curious!

Flashes of ultraviolet blue sparkled among dazzling silver and pink light as the little being zipped past my face and stopped mid-air about four feet in front of me. "Well, it's just I've had lots of time to develop and you haven't, that's all," she replied.

I had no sense she was saying she was superior to me in some way as she continued to speak, "See, we got here first. . . I'm from the first wave and you're from the second. . . we've just had more time."

"First wave? Like an ocean wave? I'm afraid I don't understand." Tiny, delicate bells were ringing somewhere. . . then, I realized it was her laughter I was hearing.

"Well, I guess you could say it is like the waves of the sea. But, really, it's just that a group of us came first and now another group is in the process of coming to Earth. You're with the second group."

"Oh. O.K." Good, I understood. I'm glad we got that settled. Then a sudden surge of energy powered my next question, "Wait a minute! Came from where? Daniel told me Earth people did not come from anywhere else."

"I don't think he said that. . . probably he said the only bodies you have ever had were on the Earth," she said, glints of gold and pale green shooting out in front of me.

"Well, now that you mention it, he did put it that way." Now, I had no idea what she had meant. I shrugged my shoulders and stated, "I'm confused."

"I suppose you are completely confused by now!" she replied, her words filled with compassion. "Let me see if I can help. You know by now how unfortunate it is when a person thinks he is just a physical body."

I answered with the passion I was feeling, "It's a terrible mistake to think that way. . . or the variation of it, to think that you're just some kind of computer-mind, you know, a linear, logical collector of information. That's the way most people see themselves. Except for the emotions. . . we don't know what to do with them, except regard them as the enemy when they get in the way of what we want to accomplish."

I considered all I had learned, before making my next statement, "Daniel said I have three spirits. I know about Adam and all the incredible work he did to create my body and keep it running. Is the second spirit the right mind?"

The tiny light darted back and forth for a moment, before coming to a stop again. Her colors were so lovely, now like those in a drop of water on a rose petal at sunrise.

"The second spirit is not the right mind, itself, but it is what created that aspect within you. Just like your nature spirit created your physical body, the second spirit created your consciousness. I prefer to call it the natural mind, because I know your scientists have divided the physical brain into right and left hemispheres. This is different than that."

I nodded mutely and waited for her to go on.

"The people on the beach showed you what a wonderful thing natural mind can be. It is simply consciousness, or awareness that you are a being and that you are living on Gaia. Unfortunately, the second wave has developed social mind instead. Like your beautiful lakes and rivers have become polluted with awful things, your social mind has become fouled with the judgments and useless information given to you by other social minds. That social mind eclipses the subtle natural mind."

Alarmed to see her colors dim a little as she said these sad words I asked, "Are you all right?"

"I am," she replied. "It's just that I feel so distressed about Gaia." She paused and seemed to pull in more energy from somewhere. Suddenly blazing with bright orange and red, she asked, "Now, what else would you like to know?"

"Well, let's see if I understand." I took in a deep breath and said, "The second spirit created my awareness of being alive and being on the Earth. That natural mind is what I could see in the people here. . . it was so wonderful. They were filled up. . . I was so amazed by that. They didn't need to compete with each other, they were just being."

"That's right!" she said happily. "Natural mind gets everything it needs straight from the third spirit, the soul. It doesn't need to steal from Adam, or from other people."

But I had a more sobering thought. "Daniel was telling me about how social mind literally steals energy from other people. That's a pretty awful thing to consider!"

"It does make for a lot of conflict and misunderstanding among you. . . and loneliness," she replied mournfully. "When you are in social mind, you are separated from soul, from other human beings, from Gaia, and your relationship with Adam suffers tremendously."

I considered what a mess we had made of our world and then said, "I can see it would be different if we were all in natural mind. But most people don't even know about it. . . I didn't! How can I be in natural mind without getting run over by all those thieving social minds out there?"

How could I let my defenses down with such danger around me? But, it was essential that I learn how to do it. That was so clear to me now. So much of my contact with other people was about protecting myself, not losing ground, not being embarrassed or making a mistake. How could I just relax, especially now that I knew many of them had social minds who wanted to steal from me?

I realized she was another mind reader when she said, "Rick, that's the beauty of it." Her colors had calmed to subtle greens and blues mixed with silver. "When you are in natural mind, social mind cannot touch you. It cannot rob you of energy. In fact, when you are in natural mind, you will find other people start to move out of social mind themselves. It's like tapping the rim of a glass. . . soon, the other glasses in the vicinity will start singing the same note."

"That would be wonderful," I breathed. "It seems like it would have a very peaceful effect."

Pleased with my perception, she answered, "That's right! Many times without a single word, you can bring harmony into a situation. No one knows what happened, but everyone is feeling a lot better. Then, there is more room to creatively solve whatever problem you were having. But you know what?" she asked happily.

"What?"

As though whispering a secret, she said, "Many of the problems which seem so real, so terribly important, dissolve once you enter natural mind."

"Wait a minute," I said, unsure it could really be that easy. "You aren't talking about just glossing over problems by pretending they're not important. . . Let me see if I really understand you. This natural mind has a particular kind of energy which comes in from the soul. The social mind has another kind of energy which it must obtain by stealing from other people." I paused, waiting for confirmation.

"That's right," she said.

"When we're in social mind, no matter what the interaction with another person may seem to be, what's really going on is that two social minds are battling for power."

"Right."

Excitement was building within me, "And the only outcome of that kind of interaction is that someone wins and someone loses. . . and that's why we struggle so hard with one another! The energy our own social mind has is completely dependent on how good it is at winning competitions with other social minds!"

"Pretty sad, isn't it?" she said.

"It's tragic," I cried. "We have so many problems with other people because we live in the part of ourselves which does nothing but try to knock the other guy down so it can be stronger."

"When you go into natural mind, the competition stops. Problems begin to dissolve because the other person's social mind cannot steal from you. Your own social mind cannot steal from them because you inactivate its abilities when you move over into natural mind."

My heart was pounding, "And that takes care of a whole lot of problems which seemed so real when they were fueled by the desperate competition for energy!"

"That's right," she said merrily. "And the problems which remain are solved a lot easier in cooperation between natural minds, instead of competition between social minds."

Filled with amazement I cried, "The solution to our conflicts has been there all the time!"

"Right inside you!" She darted and zig-zagged back and forth in front of me like an ecstatic butterfly and said, "Isn't that wonderful!"

I was getting dizzy watching her. "Can you slow down a little? I need to understand how to do that. . . how do you get into natural mind!"

"Oh Rick, you already know the answer to that!" She stopped near my ear and I could hear a steady vibration, almost a humming sound, and then she whispered, "Look in your heart."

"O.K., O.K., I'm slow. I admit it." I was exasperated with myself. How many times did I have to hear something before it began to occur to me independently?

"You aren't meant to be slow, you know," she said, compassion filling her words.

"I'm usually quite intelligent," I replied with frustration. "I grasp new information very well, but this. . ."

"This isn't about collecting information," she stated quietly.

"No. . . no, it's about discovering who I was meant to be, isn't it?" I was filled with the realization that I had been terribly confused about that for a very, very long time.

"Yes it is, and you were never meant to be slow."

"I don't understand," I muttered.

"Well, you were meant to be fast, like me!" With that she sped back and forth, a dazzling display of light and movement, every color of the spectrum sparkling in an endless display of beauty.

"I can't do that!" I exclaimed, watching her glorious ability.

She laughed, "Not right now, but this is what you were meant to be. Rick, you are pure, quickly vibrating energy encumbered by ponderous density. That's the truth of it."

Stopping mid-air, she continued, "Your social mind is composed of tremendously slow energy and it's filled with even thicker energies you collect, really steal, from other people. Anything of truth you try to run through that system is going to get stuck in the mess and you'll never see it again. That's why it takes human beings so long to understand who they are. I told you before, you can't see anything real as long as you use just your senses. The same is true about social mind. Its capacity for knowing the truth is just about zero."

I needed some hope, "But natural mind can understand it, right?"

"Of course," she replied. "Natural mind was supposed to provide an open channel from the soul directly to Adam and the person in the lifetime on Earth. But the second wave took a terrible left turn, so to speak, and developed the social mind which isn't connected to anything at all except things on the outside. That's why you are all so desperate. You're starving to death."

Heart sinking, I asked, "What do you mean?"

"Well, you have to get what you need outside of yourself because you're disconnected from the source of all energy, the source of your being." Her voice filled with sadness, she said, "When people start to run out of food, they panic. They do all sorts of things to ensure their survival."

I knew there was something else we could do. "The natural mind can get all the energy we need!"

She laughed joyfully at my realization. "That's right. Rick, just look down again."

I did as I was told and found myself staring once again at the beauty contained within my chest. There it was, the magnificent ball of shimmering, glorious light. Divided by translucent walls into chambers, it turned slowly.

"What makes that center turn, Rick?" she asked.

I answered quickly, "Those walls inside the ball."

"No," she said patiently. "They facilitate the movement. But like a water wheel, something must push against those walls to cause them to turn."

Once again, I was astounded at the splendor within me. Tiny spheres of rose and gold colored light danced, flowed, drifted inside each chamber. "I can see lots of moving light in there. Actually, it looks like particles of light pouring in from somewhere."

"Where do you suppose it's coming from?" She asked, with a touch of amusement in her voice.

I suddenly remembered, "It's energy straight from my soul. It's the tangible energy that comes right into me from the soul! You told me to look in my heart for how to get to natural mind. Is this my natural mind! Is that what you are telling me?"

"It's an essential part of it," she replied.

"This energy is meant to fuel my life, isn't it?" I said excitedly. "This area in my heart should work just like that water wheel and I'm supposed to keep it open, unclogged with debris, so the water can get where it needs to go. And I need to stand right next to that wheel so I can feel that wonderful, pure, energy coming in! That's natural mind, me standing next to that water wheel. . . not letting myself get stuck in some awful, dark little room with an obnoxious, worried jerk telling me that's all there is to life."

I felt gloriously free in this moment. I had found the fountain of life and it was right inside me! "This is wonderful! I'm so beautiful! Look, just look!"

Radiant beams of light shot out from my heart and the little voice began to laugh like a thousand tiny windchimes in a soft summer breeze. "You are beautiful! That's what we've been trying to tell you! Rick, you are beauty itself." Her light spun around mine and I was filled with love beyond my greatest imagination.

"More, Rick. Come on! You can do it!" Her voice was exhilarated, delighted, filled with love, "Let more come through. . . it's all there waiting for you to open the way! It's all there for you. Let it in, make the room, let yourself be what you were meant to be!"

I felt I could do anything and I simply let go and opened my heart as wide as I could. Like a mighty river goes over a waterfall, powerful energy poured into my heart, sparkling, radiant, strong; it spun the wheel faster and faster. I was delirious with joy and opened myself even wider. More and more came, and my body and mind disappeared in the torrent of beauty. I was pure jubilation, clear and clean, unencumbered, free!

And the humming sound came again and I knew this time it was Gaia herself. And I looked to see her beside me, spectacular heart center running smooth and fast, tremendous power and love propelling life itself forward, filling each creature and plant with pure love. We spun together, waterfalls of light and glory, and sang the song of Earth and I did not care if I ever found "Rick" again.

Chapter 24

"The thing is, you have to know who you really are and stay on the Earth at the same time! I know that's hard. That's why people who get out of social mind end up being called crazy. . . the other social minds don't like it when somebody starts telling people what's outside that little room. You know how they are, scared of getting ended. That's how they fight back."

That's Daniel, I thought. The last I could remember, I was in an enormous dance of love with Gaia. Now, I was lying face down on the ground, head supported by my arm. The earth was fragrant and warm. Opening my eyes and looking up, I could see short legs in front of me. My eyes went higher to see the red swimming trunks, little pot-belly and familiar smiling face.

"Daniel!" I exclaimed. "Where have you been? I had the most wonderful experience!" I was so happy to see him. Looking around, it appeared we were still somewhere in Hawaii.

"We're not in Hawaii," he said, again making it clear he had no difficulty reading my mind.

"I know. I know," I responded, "but close enough. I mean, we haven't gone somewhere completely different from where we met the men on the beach and I was talking to that, that. . . that little light?" I struggled to sit up.

"Nope," he said and began to walk away.

"Wait a minute!" I cried, climbing to my feet. "Wait. Where are we going?"

"Come this way. I'll show you!" I had sure heard that phrase many times today. Was it still today? Had my airplane landed a long, long time ago without me on board? Had they launched an international search for the

124

man who had mysteriously disappeared over the Atlantic? Whether it was still today or not, it really did not matter. I was never going to be the same again, that was clear. And with that realization off we went, deep into the jungle.

Pushing back giant, deep green leaves hanging out over the narrow path, I followed behind my small friend. The very air had a sense of mystery here, as the overhanging botanical majesty began to diminish the sun. Birds were everywhere, now bright yellow, then a flash of red or blue. Flowers sent out their perfume like long lost lovers and the earth beneath my feet was red and damp.

Hoping to see my new, color-flashing friend, I looked deep into the greenery. Here and there, I thought I saw a bit of sparkling light, but it was gone in the blink of an eye. I thought about my conversation with her and wondered where she was. . . what she was. "A human being of the first wave," she had said. I wanted to know more.

"Daniel, where do human beings come from?" I was struck with amusement at my own question. After all, shouldn't the seven year old be asking the adult where people come from? I hoped his explanation would be as simple as an anatomy lesson, but I knew it would not.

"From the unity, of course," he replied. Without even a pause, he continued to march down the path.

I studied his small back and steady pace and searched for a way to understand what he had said. Finding none I asked, "The unity? What's that?"

Without turning around he answered, "Where all the souls are one. . . no separation, no density, nothing but pure love. That's where you all came from in the first place. But gosh, that was an awfully, awfully, awfully long time ago!" He raised his short arms out to his sides and then dropped them in an attitude of frustration and continued to walk without looking back.

I struggled to understand what he was trying to tell me, "You mean heaven? Humans souls live in heaven until we are born, then we live on the Earth and when we die, we go back to heaven, right?" That was basically what I had thought in those middle of the night, "try to figure out where we come from," conversations with myself.

"Nope." We had come to a small clearing and Daniel stopped to look up at me. "Gaia came from heaven, but I'm afraid the souls of human beings left there a long, long time ago. Like I keep telling you, you got lost. . . really, really lost."

It seemed like a very good idea to sit down. I found myself on a patch of spongy moss and intently watched Daniel, waiting to see if he was going to offer more information without my asking. But, he had gotten diverted by a gorgeous, crimson hibiscus blossom. Stroking it carefully, he murmured softly, "Gaia, you make the most beautiful things."

"Daniel," I called. "Can you talk to me about this? Please don't leave me hanging at this point! Gaia is a being, not a rock, I sure know that now. But are you telling me there are different kinds of souls or something?"

"Well, kind of, sort of, not exactly." He came and sat down next to me. "The souls of all the human beings and Gaia used to live together in the unity. But then something so incredibly horrible happened, nobody can get over it yet and it's been millions of years!"

Chapter 25

"What!" I blurted out the question, not sure I could handle the answer.

"Yep. That's how long human beings have been lost." He looked at me with an apparent expectation that I would understand. I did not understand at all.

"Are you telling me we got lost from heaven somehow?" I said, heart beginning a familiar polka in my chest. "Are you saying we haven't been there for millions of years? Daniel, how could that be!" This was the most shocking thing I had learned all day. How could we have gotten lost from heaven?

"Well, all souls have free will, even in the unity," he began matter of factly. "And some souls a long time ago decided to use that free will and go in a different direction from the rest. They didn't mean to do anything harmful, but they just wanted to go a different way. So, they did and it caused an awful mess. And, we're still trying to get everybody to come home." Very earnestly, he looked across at me. "Any other questions?"

"Any other questions!" I cried. "Daniel, are you kidding? Where did all of these souls go? Why can't they just go back with the others if that's what everybody wants?" Unconsciously, I had leaped to my feet. "Lost from heaven, that's horrible!"

"It has been tremendously sad," Daniel said softly. "We have tried so hard to bring you all home. But once you developed social mind, you could hardly hear us at all. How can we bring you home if you don't hear us?" He gazed up at me, waiting for an answer that I could not provide.

I was suddenly horrified, "Daniel, oh my God, are you saying that story in the Bible about Lucifer and the fall from heaven is true? Are we those souls that went with the devil?"

"It's all right, Rick," he said, reaching out to pat my leg. "That's just another one of those misunderstandings. . . you didn't go with any devil and you weren't cast out of heaven. It's just you all took action which hurt everyone. You didn't mean to cause harm."

Feeling frantic I asked, "Where are the souls of human beings if they aren't in heaven?" Were we just floating around out there somewhere, hopelessly lost forever?

"Well, over millions of years, what happened was that the souls forgot who they were and where they came from." He watched me for a moment, trying to determine whether I could take any more. Apparently deciding there was a little room, he continued, "They started getting a lot of density. They stayed together in a, well a kind of. . . well, they stayed together in a chunk."

"A chunk!" I exclaimed, feeling far from comforted. "Daniel, are you saying the souls of human beings aren't in heaven, they're in some kind of lost chunk?"

"Yep." With that, he stood up and looked at me, enormous compassion shining from his eyes.

I choked out my question, "What's going to happen to us. . . how can we ever get home?"

To my surprise, his answer sounded quite cheerful, "That's why Gaia decided to come in the first place, to give the lost souls a place to have lifetimes so they could remember and drop their density and return home! That's why she did that. . . isn't that wonderful?"

"Well, yes it is, but I don't think we're getting it!" I cried, feeling desperate about our predicament. "With all I've learned today, it seems like we're getting more density, not less. We can't even hear our own souls any more."

Tears began to fall as I realized what had resulted from our confusion and my new heart seemed unable to bear the pain. "Gaia. . . Gaia, my God, we're killing her. Daniel, this is terrible!"

"Well," he said gently, "that's why we decided to show somebody. . . that's you! Like I told you, every time a teacher comes to Earth, a few people listen and then the social minds come in and tell them not to believe anything they can't measure and that's the end of it." His eyes clouded and he muttered, "Or the human beings kill him."

"Like Jesus. . ." I knew exactly what he meant. After all, I had lived through the assassinations of President Kennedy, Bobby Kennedy, Martin Luther King, Medger Evers. I knew of Mahatma Gandhi, the Tibetan monks, the Christian martyrs. It was true, the peacemakers, the revolutionaries of the heart were attacked mercilessly. First they were discredited, then they were threatened and finally, they were murdered. When I was ready to hear more I asked, "So, our very souls are encumbered by density? But, I thought we could count on that soul to give us love. . . the energy through the wheel."

"You can, Rick," he said brightly. "Even as heavy as they are by comparison to what they were, they are still much, much lighter than you are. Even as they are, they are still much closer to those energies of love."

"What do they need us for, Daniel? Why do we exist at all?" Somewhere along the line, I had started pacing. I stopped and looked at the little boy for a solution to this age-old question.

His face softened and he answered, "You're very, very important. But see, you are supposed to be like a servant to your soul. You are sent here to gather up certain lessons, particular information and bring it back to the soul for its learning. That's how it makes progress. Like a fishing net comes out from a boat to gather fish, you're supposed to bring back important experiences."

"I'm supposed to help my soul? I didn't know it needed anything. I thought it was perfect!" This was certainly a revolutionary idea to me. I had always thought my soul would help me, if I could just contact it somehow. It had never occurred to me that I might be of some use to it.

"Yep," he nodded. "You can help a lot. And, your soul is perfect. . . it just needs to get free again. That's where you come in, thanks to Gaia. See, she saw you lost out there and couldn't stand it, so she opened a school, kind of. Personality selves can come to gather up the information needed by the soul and be like those fishing nets. But, when you created social mind, you quit listening to your soul and kind of went off in your own way."

"So, we don't get the job done and the soul has to send out another personality in another body?" This was truly a tragedy of epic proportions. This went way beyond Moses getting exiled to the desert for forty years.

"Yep," he replied shrugging his shoulders. "Over and over and over again."

"I guess reincarnation is true, after all." That sure stuck in my throat. I didn't want to believe all of those stories people had been boring me with for years about their dramatic past-life experiences.

"Yep," he said, before deciding to modify his statement. "Well, kind of. People get awfully interested in what they were doing in past lifetimes, but it really doesn't matter at all. Your lifetime is just like a coat for the soul. . . a temporary covering. Studying past lives is like devoting a lot of time to looking at all the coats you've ever owned in your whole life."

I understood what he was saying. "So, if personalities and bodies are just temporary coverings, but we forget and go our own way, it's just like if a coat were to walk out of my hall closet and decide to take off on its own!"

Daniel was giggling, "Yep. . . pretty funny. Especially if the coat thought it was real and you weren't and wouldn't listen to you. And what if it got really, really cold and you needed that coat and it wouldn't come back!"

"Like the soul needs us to use this lifetime to gather what it needs to go home?" I didn't think this was so funny. After all, we had been lost for a very long time. We needed to get our act together and quit fooling around.

There were left over pieces to my puzzle. "But Daniel, that little non-fairy person, she said she was human. . . the first wave. . . she was so different. These first and second waves, what's that all about?"

He answered quickly, "It's just that there are so many lost souls, Gaia asked that they be given lifetimes in two groups, so that she could help them better. . . you know, not get overwhelmed. So, you were talking to one of the human beings who came into physical form with the first group." Looking away for a moment, he added, "I'm afraid they did a lot better with their opportunity than you guys are doing."

Sadly, I had no evidence to the contrary, but an interesting thought occurred to me. I had thought that little light was a fairy. Maybe that was the answer to all of the legends about fairies and little people all over the world. Maybe they were humans of the first wave!

The child grinned happily and answered my unspoken question, "Yep, those legends are true, Rick!"

I would never get over being startled every time he did that. "Daniel, I do wish you wouldn't do that! How can I keep anything private from you?"

"Can't," he replied simply. "I can hear everybody all the time anyway. . . all over the Earth. You all mostly sound the same, I'm afraid. Lots of worries and fears, not much love."

I considered that for a moment before continuing my pursuit, "Anyway, so what we call fairies, those are real?" Wow, I liked that idea a lot. I started to smile.

"Yep. Well, kind of. They don't have wings and all that stuff. But, some of them occupied the Earth at the same time as the second wave people."

After all I had been through today, the fact that these incredible, magical beings had really existed, after all, came as a joyful piece of information. "So, the little people. . . the Irish leprechauns, those menehunes my friend talks about, the trolls the German people speak of, the elves of the Dutch. . . those were first wave beings, too?"

"Yep. Well, of course the stories told about them are all mixed up. But they did really live on the Earth." He said the next words with a great deal of sadness. "See, the more you poison Gaia, the fewer first wave beings there are. . . they leave because they can't breathe in the middle of all the density."

We were so terribly lost, we had even managed to send a lot of the magic out of our world. I wanted to know why we were so different, "Why was the first wave group so successful, Daniel, and we're having such a hard time?"

His answer came with compassion, "Partly, because you spent a much longer time in the chunk. . . and partly it's just a result of free will. See, people can always make a choice to set down density or pick up some more. Unfortunately, once a lot start to pick it up, they teach others to do the same. Before you know it, everybody's lost. Besides that, the first wave never developed social mind. Isn't that the most beautiful creature?" Suddenly, he scrambled off, chasing after an iridescent, blue butterfly.

A protest died at my lips and I decided to scamper after him. We allowed the innocent daughter of Gaia to lead us where she would. Running back and forth, eyes heavenward, following this bit of color on the wind, now right above us, now drifting out of sight like a dream, she pulled us well away from the path and having done so, disappeared completely.

Chapter 26

I looked around, unable to find any sense of direction. Giant ferns, wrapped by enormous vines surrounded me and the verdant canopy above was so thick, I could not see the sky. It began to rain, warm water showering down over my body. Lifting my face, I allowed myself to be cleansed before returning to my concern about where I was.

"Daniel, where are we?" Somehow, I knew he was not going to be there even before the interminable silence confirmed it. Why does he insist on doing that? I wondered, only half anxiously. Pulling fragrant red berries from one of the vines, I decided there were far worse places to be stranded. The luscious, sweet fruit filled my senses as I looked into the seemingly impassable greenery. With a measure of relief I considered the fact that this time, Daniel had disappeared without anything strange happening. I decided to just sit down and relax for awhile.

This really was a wonderfully beautiful place. I wished that I knew more about plants, these were certainly spectacular. The tip of a lush leaf brushed my arm and I was amazed to see it was actually bigger than my torso. That butterfly really led us deep into the jungle, I thought. This is a place where things have had a chance to grow undisturbed for a very long time. I stroked the stem of an odd, bright green, slightly hairy plant, and seeing how very delicate it was, wondered how far away I was from the ocean. Maybe Daniel was just giving me an opportunity to rest; I certainly deserved it. I stretched my legs out and reached for some more fruit, comfortable to have nothing to do for awhile.

How was I ever going to get home? I smiled a little with the realization that term now had two meanings. I did want to get home to my family and friends, but I had a new desire. I wanted to go home to "the unity," as Daniel had called it. And to be perfectly honest about it, I wanted more of the intensely moving experiences I had been having recently.

My fingers ran lightly over the grass by my side and I remembered to thank Gaia, just as Daniel had done. She really did make magnificent things. I wondered about the theories of evolution. . . certainly man did not develop from the apes, as I had learned in school. Daniel had told me very advanced human beings were running around on the planet a very, very long time ago. And what about plants? Did Gaia just randomly create what she wished? Did science really know anything about it?

Suddenly, I heard sounds in the jungle. Far away, they still seemed very loud. What on Earth could make such a noise? I jumped to my feet as they became closer. It seemed the very jungle itself was shaking. The horrible sound of trees falling was added to by the sight of giant ferns being smashed. The Earth was moving under a tremendous force. I placed my feet far apart to secure my balance and frantically looked for a place to run to get out of the way. It must be a bulldozer, I thought, adrenalin coursing through my body. Wait a minute, they didn't have machines like that 720,000 years ago. What the hell was going on?

A moment ago, everything had been in perfect balance, now magnificent living things were being pulverized, ground into the Earth. Green liquid oozed out of the formerly impeccable plants and the red berries ran like blood over my feet. Terrified about my own safety, I was astounded at the destruction of the beauty around me. How could this happen? Damn developers don't have a clue about the environment, I thought as I searched for higher ground. I'm going to let them know they could have killed somebody out here.

Now the approaching sound was a roar and I had found no way to secure my safety. I'm going to have to just stand right here and hope they see me. Pulling myself up to my greatest height, I was fueled with a righteous anger, determined to make my opinion known. Bulldozers in paradise, what a tragedy. Couldn't human beings leave anything alone?

An incomprehensible sound reached my ears. An immense, rumbling noise detonated directly over my head. What was left of the green life around me withered as the sounds continued to reverberate above me. What could that be? What kind of an aircraft could make such a noise? The sound was too much to bear and, putting my hands over my ears, I searched the sky to see what was producing it. And there ten stories above me, was a man's face.

My knees gave way and I crumpled to the ground which shook violently again as this giant began to move. His feet! Oh my God, where were his feet? I looked desperately around; if he stepped on me, I would be dead in an instant! Where were those feet?

There was a sudden movement of air, like the wind being sucked out of a building in a fire. I knew I was directly in line with this monster's boot. It was all over; there was nothing I could do. Just as the plants all around me were now unrecognizable, I was going to be crushed.

"Use your abilities." The voice seemed to speak inside my head.

"I don't know how!" I cried out. "Help me, I don't know how!"

From somewhere deep within me I heard, "You know where to go. Use your abilities." But the thunderous roar of the giant continued and the foot swept down toward me like a wrecking ball follows an inevitable arc into the side of a building. Tensing my body and mind, I prepared for death.

Calmly, the voice said, "Let go, Rick. Don't constrict. Open, release, let go of it all."

"Open!" I protested violently. "Open, now? I can't, I can't!"

As the foot blocked out the light, I cried, "Help me! Please, help me!" Taking one last, deep breath, I closed my eyes and braced myself for tremendous pain.

"Oh Rick, that won't work, at all!" This was a different voice. The roaring had stopped and I dared to open my eyes. There before me was a familiar, but disappointed little face. "You really do have to start paying attention or you're going to stay lost for another million years!"

"Pay attention?" My voice sounded like bending metal and my body trembled uncontrollably. Frantically, I looked around for the foot, the giant and the jungle, but could not see them.

In fact, we did not seem to be anywhere at all. A sparkling profusion of silver, pink and pale lavender light drifted all around us and a sense of profound serenity surrounded me on all sides. Somewhere in the distance tiny bells rang and I managed to squeak out a question, "Am I dead?"

"Of course not, silly!" Daniel was filled with his usual merriment again. "You still have the same vehicle to use. But Rick, my goodness, I thought you had learned more than that."

Fear continued to crash through me as I scanned my environment for danger. "What happened? Who was that man, where did he go?"

"Just a regular human being walking around. . ." He shrugged his small shoulders and looked up at me.

The adrenalin in my body found a worthy cause and I exploded, "What the hell does that mean? Daniel, I could have been killed! Don't you care about my feelings? I was scared out of my mind! Just a regular human being. . . he was 100 feet tall!"

"86 feet." The child looked at me solemnly.

"What!" I was filled with righteous anger, "Who cares whether it was 100 feet or 86 feet? I almost died out there!"

"Actually," Daniel said matter of factly, "he was just a normal person, it was you who had changed. You were very small and he was, like I just said, just a regular human being walking around."

How could he continue to torture me like this? "Daniel, that can't be true! He was so destructive. . . trees were falling, plants were dying everywhere. It was terrible, didn't you see that?"

"That's what I'm trying to tell you, Rick. One human being, filled with density, can be a very heavy and destructive force." He waited for my response, watching me struggle to understand.

I was aghast, "You mean that's what one person does to the environment when he simply walks through it?"

"Yep," he nodded.

I could hardly believe my ears. "My God, one person has that effect even without a bulldozer? I thought the end of the world was here."

He stretched out his arms and replied, "I know. That's how it feels to everyone when a second wave human being shows up. Pretty sad, huh?"

I searched for a little hope, "Are we all like that?"

"Nope," he said with a faint smile. "He was an unfortunate example of the heaviest kind of human. . . one with a lot of density. Some of you are much lighter than that."

I shook my head, "We must have switched time zones somewhere along the way. . . I mean, he wasn't at all like those guys of the beach or that little bit of light I was talking to."

"Yep," he confirmed. "Moved back to the time where you guys live. . . quite a difference, huh?"

"An awful difference," I groaned.

"Like I said, the first wave of human beings really took better advantage of the opportunity Gaia offered than you guys are doing. . . I guess you've seen first hand now what the difference feels like to her. I mean, she was never meant to support the kind of energy that you just experienced and now, there are so many of you just like that. . . even worse!"

My God, I had never realized what an incredible burden we were to Earth. "Why, Daniel? Why are we getting heavier and heavier, as you put it? What's the matter with us?"

"Well," he said, observing my distress. "Souls are continuing to arrive from the chunk. . . that means there are lots of people on the Earth who are in their very first lifetime after eons of time being lost. I'm afraid they bring a lot of darkness with them. After all, they haven't had any opportunity at all yet to get cleansed of all the junk they accumulated."

I thought for a moment and asked, "Are you saying that the increase in violence on the Earth in recent years has to do with some kind of difference in the type of souls who are coming into bodies? It's not all sociopolitical stuff?"

"Nope. But, social minds develop around those denser souls and then you get the so. . . soci. . . soci. . . what you said." Abruptly, he started a child's dance of some sort, whirling and turning, arms outstretched he ran past me, light cascading off of his arms like water from a heron's wings.

"Daniel! Daniel, wait a minute. . . what are you doing?" I didn't want to let him out of my sight. I had no idea where I was and I had no intention of suffering through another rude solitary surprise. As he continued to move away from me, I had no choice but to follow him.

This was a wondrous place. . . the air filled with a magical electricity. On our way to who knew where, I experimented with the light flowing over the surface of my skin like the water in my shower. Loping behind the little boy, I stretched my arms out and watched the particles of silver and pink bounce from the surface of my hands and spray over my forearms like the surf hitting the rocks on the seashore.

Like an elegant schooner shooting through the waves of energy, my chest broke through sheets of windowed light, personal bow cutting its way, splitting the endless sea of silver. Showers of light shot up into the air like sparks from a campfire on a summer night's beach and drifting back downward, they swirled a spiral dance of magnificent intensity, now gold, now red and blue, silver and orange. Purple fire landed in my heart and exploded, sending volumes of tiny spheres of light out around me to multiply ten thousand fold what was already there.

"Daniel. . . this is so beautiful. Look! Look what I can do!" I was overflowing with elation, a deep, rich, luscious joy filled my every corner. The small boy turned and watched me for a moment as I managed to catch another spark with my heart and burst once again into a majestic fountain of exhilarating light.

"Rick. . . that's so good!" The little voice was delighted and I continued to play in the light like a small child on the seashore, throwing armfuls of refracting color high into the air and laughing from deep inside my being as it showered back over me.

Splashing happily in the endless supply of energy, I caught a glimpse of something out of the corner of my eye. Startled, I stopped and turned my head to view the awful spectacle before me.

Chapter 27

I could see him well ahead of me. Dazed, I began to approach in disbelief, then stopped about fifteen yards away. Filled with dread, I spoke quietly to Daniel. "Tell me what's going on. . . please just tell me. . . what. . . how can this be?"

"We just want you to watch for a little while, Rick. Just watch." His words were achingly compassionate and I did as I was told.

My heart was breaking, but I kept my eyes on the man in the bubble. He appeared to be struggling fiercely, pounding with his fists, yelling, pacing back and forth, agitated, afraid. In the midst of the spectacular field of light, he was cut off by walls of a different kind of energy. Cloudy and speckled with black and brown, this prison seemed much too small for him.

Again and again, he marched across the tiny space, flailing and crashing against its walls, sometimes falling to the floor with despair. I was desperate to help him somehow. There was so much incredible beauty surrounding him, but he did not seem to be able to see it. Caught like a prisoner in an interrogation room, this man could not see beyond his one way glass.

To my horror, the man suddenly began punching his stomach, legs and arms. As I watched him, muffled sentences reached my ears and I was appalled to hear the blasts of terrible condemnation he fired at himself. My own agitation increased beyond my ability to contain it, "Daniel, for God's sake, what's he doing in there? We can't just stand out here, we have to help him!"

"Just watch, Rick." There was an urgent sound in the child's voice that signaled it was best for me to follow his direction.

The man suddenly sat down. Holding his head in his hands, he did not move for a long time. Then, standing up again, he began to pace and push on the walls. The bubble had grown more pock-marked with dull brown and black spots during the time we had watched it. It seemed the more the man struggled, the more opaque the walls became. Soon, it appeared, we would have no view of him, at all.

"All right, Rick. It's time to go closer. He can't see you. Just go up as close as you need to. I want you to look into his face." Again, the little boy's words were tremendously compassionate. Good, I thought, at least he cares as much about this man as I do. We'll be able to do something for him. At this point, I needed to draw closer to be able to see the man at all. Like the bug-splattered windshield of a car after a long trip, the walls of the bubble were increasingly covered with obscuring debris. I crossed the remaining distance between us and put my face up against the bubble, peered inside and promptly fell backwards in shock.

"Daniel, good God!" I cried, struggling back up on my feet. I felt compelled to look inside the bubble once again and found nausea rising in my throat at the sight inside. The man continued to struggle, tears rolling down his face, but that face. . . that face was mine!

"It's all right, Rick." A quiet voice spoke beside me. "I know it's hard to look at, but I'm right here." Looking quickly around, I could see no one. The voice did not sound like Daniel's.

"It's me. . . my God, that man trapped in that bubble, it's me." Sobs broke my words apart and I could not continue for a moment. The bubble continued to be splattered with the dark substance and I could barely see the man. He had sat down again, apparently exhausted.

"How can it be? I'm here, I'm right here, but that's me over there, isn't it? It's not somebody who looks like me, it is me." I did not know whether to attend to my collapsing mind or breaking heart. I felt enormous compassion for the human being who was suffering so intensely, but my mind could not accept I could be two places at once. "What. . . what am I doing in that bubble? How did I get there?"

"You built it for yourself, Rick." The soft voice spoke again. Overflowing with kindness, there was no blame in the statement.

Protest welled up in my throat, "I built it? I have no idea what you are talking about. How could I have built something when I didn't even recognize it? And how could I be here and there at the same time?"

"Most human beings build one for themselves," the voice said quietly. I could barely see myself inside the bubble, now thickly covered with the dark material.

"What is it? Why would people build such an awful thing?" I still had no idea where we were or how I could be in two places at once. There was no movement in the bubble at all. I assumed I must be lying down again.

"It begins to happen from the day you are born. You are not welcomed as a great soul, but as a nothing which must be built up into a something."

I still had no idea who the voice belonged to. "Daniel was telling me about that a while ago, but what does that have to do with this bubble?"

Ever so gently, my instructor continued, "You see, if you are cut off from knowledge of your own being, you become lost and afraid. Those around you have long forgotten the truth of their being as well. Without this awareness, human beings become vulnerable and frightened. They begin to create protection for themselves and in doing so, create a wall between what they think of as 'me' and what in truth is 'I.'"

Perplexed I said, "I'm sorry. You've lost me."

Infinite patience permeated the next words, "You see, out of lack of knowledge and fear, each of you becomes a hardened capsule within the enormous field of the soul. The energies and wisdom of that soul continue to surround you, but you do not see them or feel them."

"Wait a minute! Are you saying that we are standing in the middle of my soul right now and that's me, stuck in some kind of capsule over there?"

"Yes, that is right."

"And I created that capsule myself, out of fear and ignorance about the reality of who I truly am?" I had no idea who I was talking to, but that didn't seem as important as rescuing myself from that polluted prison.

"Very good, Rick." The voice sounded pleased. "Your awareness has been captured inside the walls of your body and inside the walls of your senses. The reality that you worship is only a reality created by means of the limited information which comes through those senses. But, that is only a part of reality, a tiny layer in a greater existence with multiple layers. For centuries and centuries people of science have said, 'Did you see that or hear that or taste that or feel that?' They believe that only what is known through the senses is real and all else is not."

"What's all the junk on the bubble, the capsule, whatever?" I had an idea, but I was not sure.

"What do you think, Rick?" All day long, no one had been willing to just give me a simple, straight answer.

I looked again at the awful, mottled mess. "Well, I think it must be density. . . it looks thick and very different from the rest of the energy I've been seeing. It just feels heavy." The more I talked, the more sure I was of my answer.

"That is very good, Rick." The soft voice reflected genuine pleasure at my understanding.

Concerned about the other me I asked, "Why am I so upset in there? I mean, it does look like a very small space to have to live in, but he's, I'm really actively distressed. . . at least I was. I haven't seen any movement for a while, I guess he's, I've calmed down."

Sadness permeated the next words, "Most personality selves are agitated and afraid. Most attack themselves with words and self-destructive behavior. As you have seen, the more they do that, the more density is created. But often, the ones who become most agitated are like you."

"How am I different?" I wasn't sure I liked being so unique if what I was seeing was the reward for it.

"Rick, you have been trying for a long time to get out. The personality self who knows in his heart that he is separated from his greater being begins to struggle against his confinement. Unfortunately, the way he goes about it is often contrary to what needs to occur."

"I don't understand."

As if trying to calm my emotions, the voice spoke slowly, "Trying to get to spirit by running frantically from place to place, searching desperately for a special teacher or technique, a church, a group, a cause results only in valuable energy going outward. The answer is always inward."

I thought about how human beings would try anything to find meaning in their lives. Sometimes what they came up with could seem pretty strange to anyone else. But the whole time, the answer had been in the last place we would ever look.

I wondered what the result of all that running around could be. "If nothing is accomplished by looking to the outside, then what?"

The voice answered, "Personality becomes more afraid and makes a thicker and thicker capsule around itself. Without a connection to soul, it feels scared and wanders without purpose in confusion, loneliness and despair. It is only a very tiny thing with many whistles and bells, making a lot of noise in its world. But it knows deep inside, it is not the totality of your being. Its little kingdom in the capsule is only an illusion. Knowing this, it becomes even more afraid and constricts and hardens even more."

I already knew what that meant. "And all that fear and constriction makes for even more density."

"Absolutely. In fact, fear acts as a magnet for density and the person becomes even more separated from the field of his true being."

"What happens then?"

Quietly, the voice replied, "Personality marches back and forth in its capsule with great energy, trying desperately to get all aspects of life on Earth in order, thinking it will then feel safe."

"And the more energy it diverts into that, the less it uses to reconnect with his soul?" I knew that one. I had created diverse projects all my life. Whenever I felt existential anxiety, I started something new and didn't have to think about it for a while. Sometimes it didn't even matter whether the new venture failed or not. Either way, it was a comforting diversion.

There was tremendous love in every word the voice spoke, "You see, no safety can ever come from outside things. Personality knows that, but avoids thinking about it by creating more and more to do on the outside. All things on Earth are limited, they come to an end. Placing your safety on something which by definition will not always be there makes for great fear."

"And a lot of middle of the night anxiety attacks," I said sadly.

Softly I heard, "Personality is not as successful in the night at avoiding the awareness of the fact that it is a limited being with a finite end, as are all things which are part of its world."

"Boy, we try hard to avoid thinking about that!" I considered how much energy and time people put into finding just the right relationship; the one that would be there for all time. And jobs. . . everyone was frantic about their security. We were so frightened about our own mortality and yet we were faced with the evidence of our own demise every day.

"Why doesn't the soul just prevent all of that?" After all, it seemed terribly heartless to allow us to become so lost and unhappy.

"Remember, Rick. Earth must always be a place of absolute free will. The moment your soul sends you forth into the Earthtime, you are free to do what you wish. Your soul will not knock on your capsule and demand that you stop separating yourself. It will sit and wait for you to dissolve the capsule that keeps you apart."

"Even if we make an absolute mess out of our lives?" I didn't want to give up the idea that something was magically going to rescue me someday from my responsibility to find solutions to my own dilemmas.

The voice continued to explain, "The energies of the soul are subtle, fine and soft, and they will not wear away density. Personality has slower energies, the kind that can contact density. You see, asking soul to wear down density is like expecting air to tumble down a stone wall that a man has built. Like the soul, the air is patient and will wait and surround it, even permeate it, even softly caress it and follow its every line and curve and crevice but it cannot knock the wall down."

"So, are you saying it's up to us to do something about our separation from our own soul? Like Daniel told me, just passively calling out to God or angels or some kind of cosmic problem-solver isn't really going to help at all."

"That is correct."

"How do I do it? Tell me, how can I get myself out of that horrible jail cell?" I watched the bubble for any signs of movement. It had been a long time since I had seen any sign of life there.

The voice answered, "First, personality, the part you think of as 'me', must begin to define itself as an accessory, a tool, an instrument of the soul. That is why you were given a physical body and sent into the Earthtime. Instead of acting like an emperor in a tiny, illusionary kingdom inside the capsule, it must see itself as an essential part of something tremendously important, vast and glorious.

"You see, it is the role of personality to bring back the experiences of the Earthtime for the soul's progression. But it is also its role to bring the light of the soul down into the relative darkness of your Earth. Like a beacon shines in the black night, so can your personality broadcast the pure light of your soul out through the density surrounding Earth."

I murmured, "That sounds so beautiful. . . and so important."

"It is, Rick. Particularly in this time of great distress for Gaia and the increasing confusion of the second wave beings. Many are searching. . . the light of your soul coming through a personality in alignment with that soul can help others to find their way as well."

I was searching for some way out of the mistakes I had made, "So, the first step is to practice thinking of myself as an instrument of something much bigger and more important."

Gently, the voice responded, "That is true. . . you must begin to see yourself as a possession of the soul."

"And my lifetime as being important to the growth of that soul?" That would sure lend a lot more meaning to my existence! I had always wondered what I was doing here. I think we all wonder that at some point. After all, making money, buying things and competing for recognition was pretty meaningless when you considered the fact that it all comes to a frightening end.

"And what else is important in order to reconnect with the greater field of your being?" the voice asked quietly.

"I don't know. . ." I thought for a second before I remembered the obvious, "Yes I do know! Getting rid of as much density as I possibly can . . . making choices moment by moment to lessen, rather than increase the density."

"Very good, Rick."

I went on, "And not feeding that social mind thing. That's what was splattering density all over the walls of my capsule, wasn't it? All that agitated confusion was social mind darting here and there, trying to get free and making itself a stronger prison the whole time!"

The voice added, "Social mind is a prolific producer of density, I'm afraid."

"Well, that makes sense because it prevents me from knowing who I really am, and that makes for fear and that creates a lot of decisions and behavior based on that fear which just makes a thicker wall which just makes more fear and more desperation!" My sentences were starting to sound like Daniel's, but it did not matter. I understood! I understood!

"Rick, personality generates many illusions. . . what picture must it present today so that it can win over its fellow human beings. It must win because it must have energy. The energy must come from outside because it has no source inside."

So much made sense to me now. "The more the world gets cut off from soul, the more desperate we are. . . that's part of the reason for all the terrible violence, isn't it?"

144

The voice answered, "As long as you see your own personality self as real and think only in terms of the concerns of that personality, as long as you have little connection with your soul, so you will see other personalities as well. When one lost personality, detached in awareness from its soul encounters another detached personality, there is great potential for physical and psychological violence."

"Because we don't see the whole picture. . . we don't see the fact that everyone is an enormous field of energy. We just see some little guy out there trying to take what we desperately need for ourselves. Depending on how frantic we get about what we don't have, we'll do anything to that guy to get it."

I had thought about this before in economic terms. Like the man who can't get a job gets desperate and ends up committing a crime in order to eat. Then, he's on that road and doesn't know how to fix it and becomes more desperate and keeps victimizing others so he can survive. But this was much wider than that. . . this involved everybody, not just a particular segment of society.

Overflowing with compassion, the voice responded, "All conflicts between human beings have one place of resolution and that is in the consciousness of each person, not in the interplay between the two. When detached personality selves are busy in their little kingdoms comparing and competing, playing bigger and smaller, stronger and weaker, it can truly seem that the only place to resolve interpersonal problems is on the outside. Humans look at one another and social mind tries to find a way to win. It thinks about how it can knock another down, verbally, even physically. It plots to find something to do to the other person to gain what it needs. It tries to manipulate and argue the other person out of his position.

"But, the only place of resolution is within each being. . . acknowledge yourself as the spiritual being that you truly are. . . acknowledge the spiritual reality of the other being. . . know that his personality is a temporary device, as is yours. Practice seeing you are both creations of spirit. See the beauty of the soul who sits across from you, even as personality plays grotesque games of power. In this way, conflict with another person can simply be a string around your finger to remind you of your own spiritual work."

Excitement was building inside me, "So, we're all trapped in these little spaces, bubbles, capsules, really tombs! We're supposed to be part of an enormous being, not just what our senses can measure."

"Very good."

I didn't want to be contained in a tiny space. "What else can I do to get free?"

"Begin your practice of setting down the density. Begin to practice knowing the truth of what your lifetime is all about. This will begin to create a tiny hole, a way out of your entombment. You have been buried alive, you have been placed in a lifeless tomb. You must wish with all your heart to claw your way out and into freedom for you are alive! You can realize that you exist not only within the boundaries of this body, but outside it as well. You can realize that you exist beyond the boundaries of what was taught to you and you exist outside the boundaries of all the things you have seen and touched and tasted and heard."

I could feel passion rising within me. I did not want to remain buried alive! I wanted out of my prison. I wanted to reclaim my existence. All of it! "I want to get out!" I said, emotion charging my words with a voltage unfamiliar to me.

"That's right, Rick! It is from within you that the cry for freedom must come. No one can give this to you. No one can say, 'Take my passion and use it.' From deep within you must come the desperate demand to reclaim who you are."

Everything was clear in this moment. Like those special days when the light is absolutely perfect and everything in the environment is sharp and full, I could see what was being said. Why hadn't people known this before? Why hadn't we stood up and demanded our birthright?

"What takes us so long to get to this point? We've been robbed by our own social minds! Why have we settled for this kind of existence?" I asked indignantly.

"Like anything which loses its freedom, first you did protest and shout, then came desperation and the frantic demand to be free. But once something is trapped long enough, it will resign itself to what seems to be fate and forget what is true."

I remembered reading somewhere about the fact that if you keep flies in a jar with a lid on it, after awhile you can remove that lid and the flies will not go beyond the top of the jar. They have learned they cannot get past a certain point. Once they learn to be trapped, they stay trapped.

Clearly, the voice had read my mind when it said the next words, "If you practice continually remembering the truth of your being and focus an undying passion and desire on the goal of breaking free, you will grow bigger than your capsule. You can be a butterfly, with personality as the little bug in the middle and soul the beautiful wings that make it fly. And if you keep going, you will find yourself at once with beautiful colored wings on either side, lifting you as high as you wish to go and as far as you wish to fly. . .''

My heart was already flying. I could be free again! I did not have to be trapped in what we all called the human condition. None of us had to stay in those horrible prisons of our own making. I didn't know exactly how I was going to do it yet. But I could learn and I was ready to do whatever it took. No one could afford to be passive any longer. We all had to break for freedom! It was time to stand up again and reclaim our truth and in doing so, we had only our illusions to lose and limitless love and energy to gain.

I bent down and scooped up a huge handful of glorious golden light and sent it straight up into the air and yelled with all the power I could find in my being, "I want it! I want it back! It's mine and I want it back!"

With that, the ugly mottled bubble cracked and fell open and the man unfurled himself and filled with an awesome beauty, stepped out into the magnificent field of light.

Chapter 28

"Hi!" Turning around quickly, I was astounded to see Daniel walking toward me, gold and silver light bouncing from his bare feet. "You're out of the bubble! That's so good, Rick!"

"It's wonderful!" I exclaimed. "I don't quite understand how I did that, but it is wonderful."

On the news, I had seen rehabilitated eagles being released back into the wild. I had silently cried as I saw a crated symbol of freedom carried off a truck and up a forest trail. I imagined its fear at being so hopelessly caught in the hands of the dangerous strangers, their kind having been responsible for its injuries. But at last the moment would come, door sweeping open the bird would peer outside, scarcely believing it could go home again. Then, with a magnificent wild cry and a burst of its wings, away it would go, joy raining down from the sky as it left its sorrow and sent itself rushing heavenward. I knew now why my tears had come.

Daniel looked at me solemnly and said, "Let's see if you can stay out."

I could hardly believe my ears. "What do you mean? Once I'm out, I'm out. Right?" I found a deep sadness in the pit of my stomach that I now realized had been there for a very long time. Now that I was free, I did not ever want to end up like that again.

"Nope." He had a way of saying the most difficult things with a single word.

"You mean I could get trapped all over again?" I already knew the answer.

Very slowly, he spoke one enormously frightening word, "Yep."

I felt like a slave who had broken free only to find his captors waiting in the dark, having known of his plan the whole time. "Please Daniel, come on, help me out a little. How could that happen?"

"Remember how tricky social mind was?" He said, kicking up effervescent beams with his foot. Spectacular blue, violet and orange particles of light flew high into the air and floated back to ground. I could not help but notice the terrible comparison between this beauty and the ugliness of that capsule.

"Yes, of course I do, " I responded with a vehemence which surprised even me. "It's responsible for so much human misery. I know that now."

"It can sneak right up on you and before you know it," he clapped his hands forcefully together, "you're trapped."

"So, sounds like I have to keep watching out for it all the time." All right, if that's what I needed to do, so be it. I was not going back, not now.

"Yep. Really, you just have to remember all the time that it's there. Don't let it get away with anything. Don't let it ramble on with anything it wants to. The minute something comes into your head that is hurtful for you or someone else. . . you know, stuff that's a judgment or a comparison of some kind. If it isn't positive, throw it right out! See, if you let the social mind get its hands on something yucky, it will multiply it. And, I don't think you can afford to let even one splatter of gunk start spreading."

"God, I could see how awful it was. When I was in the bubble, that dark stuff just keep getting thicker and thicker, until I couldn't even see myself in there any more. . . and I'm sure I couldn't see out."

And I remembered the tragic desperation I witnessed. It was far worse than anything I had seen before. No wonder we suffer emotionally and physically. No wonder most of us don't dare to say how very unhappy we are inside.

Daniel nodded at me sadly, "You miss even seeing your own soul, let alone being with it, like you are right now."

"This is so incredibly wonderful, Daniel. I want to have it for the rest of my life." Even with the sadness and fear I was experiencing at even a mention of the idea that I could find myself back in the capsule if I wasn't careful, I had never felt so full of joy as I did right now. In the midst of my own vast soul, there was profound beauty everywhere. And love, safety, security. . . what I was being given no human being could hope to provide. Nothing I could ever gain from another person, nothing I could feel from any accomplishment I might generate, nothing I could ever produce could even approach this happiness. That's what I wanted now. Anything else, no matter how grand social mind might think it was, would be only an empty reminder of how far away I had sent my soul.

The little boy looked at me a moment and said, "See, you don't really have to make social mind an enemy. . . it's more that you honor yourself by keeping yourself clean. . . you know, you wouldn't let your body get all mucked up day after day and not wash it."

"Of course not," I replied, making a face at the thought of being so dirty.

"Same thing."

O.K., so I didn't have to live in a state of war with the social mind. I, after all, had the real power if I would just consistently keep it. I had seen that was true by my experience with that miserable little mean man inside me. Once I had stood up and told him in no uncertain terms to stop, he had obeyed. But, I also remembered he had attacked Adam for energy the first chance he got.

A wonderful thought occurred to me, "You said something about bringing that light into life on Earth. . . for other people?"

"Yep. See, when you are clear and clean, your soul's energy begins to shine right through you, just like the way you were on the beach. Weren't you beautiful? Don't you think it would be great for some of this light to be in the world?" He bent over and sent handfuls tiny, emerald and gold incandescent spheres raining down over us.

That light was glorious. My skin was again transparent, my heart turning and light flowing from me in every direction. I remembered how it had lit up the darkness as nothing else could. "It could help other people. . . and Gaia, too."

A smile crossed his face as he answered, "Yep. See, that's the difference between keepers making big speeches about spirit and having nothing change. You know what? It's just as easy for social mind to use spirituality as a subject to make itself stronger as it is for it to use something else."

I considered a peculiar thought I had never shared with anyone. Taking a breath, I said, "Well, now that you mention it, spiritual people have always been kind of a pain in the neck. I hate to say that, but. . . do you know what I mean?" What was it? Spiritual people always looked superior somehow, like the cat who swallowed the canary, above the rest of us. It was maddening. Over the years, I had learned how to "look spiritual" when necessary, but I didn't really have it inside.

Now I understood, the people who were coming across that way didn't have it either. It was just social mind with another script, another strategy by which to grab energy. I could imagine how successful that particular ploy could be. While I was busy feeling spiritually inadequate, their social mind was stealing energy from Adam like crazy. That why I felt such dread when the topic came up! It had all been a sham the whole time, just another social mind exercise in seeing who could be strongest and biggest.

Daniel broke into my thoughts, "Rick, you're doing so well!"

I was excited, feeling I might actually be on my way to permanent liberation. "Daniel, are you saying if social mind is out of the way, we would actually be able to consistently offer each other the kind of love which exists right here in the soul?"

"Of course you could, that's the whole point!" He grinned at me enthusiastically.

"And, correct me if I'm wrong, but we wouldn't have to necessarily say a single word about anything spiritual at all, would we?" My heart was beginning to pound with a new vision of the world beginning to appear in my mind.

"Nope." He continued to smile.

Now I was smiling, too. "But that's a revolutionary idea! All of this has absolutely nothing to do with pious words, or threats of punishment or praying hard enough or believing scripture or any of that! And it doesn't have to do with calling to angels to come and save us. It's all personal work, isn't it? The whole thing all this time has been about battling social mind and breaking free into the surrounding field of our own soul!"

"Yep," he nodded.

"Daniel, that could change everything!" I said, barely able to contain myself.

After all, what could happen if all the churches turned into centers for learning about how to get rid of social mind, instead of posturing halls for that social mind? Suppose ministers learned how to really access their own soul energies, instead of pretending they understood a whole bunch of esoteric material that was cruel, even bloody in nature? And what if we could gather together and simply fill ourselves and each other up with those tangible energies of love like the men on the beach had offered me? If that vengeful Earth god was removed from our shoulders and we took back our own power. . . my God, nothing would ever be the same again!

"Daniel you're talking about a whole new chance for mankind! If social mind is removed from power and we all learn to be what we were meant to be, everything would change! All those directions for living that were so garbled up, we could replace them with energies of the soul. . . can you imagine what kinds of communities we could create together! That old dream of caring for each other, making sure no one went hungry, knowing how much we are all loved and never forgotten. My God, that's possible, isn't it?"

"Yep. That's what we've tried so hard to tell you all along." He continued with renewed seriousness, "But I have to tell you, social mind is a terrible opponent. It kills the teachers and hides the truth. It demands that things be proven in the realm of density."

"You're talking about how we don't trust anyone who tries to help us sort all this out. We always want to see a miracle of some kind. A mountain moving, instant cures to disease, things like that?"

I had felt that way myself. But other social minds were out there, willing to capitalize on that need. So many so-called ministries were all about desperate people looking for proof that God exists. I thought about a recent news report which said a thousand people had tried to barge into someone's backyard because they had heard a report that a voice was coming out of the hot tub there. It wasn't that the voice was saying anything helpful or profound, it was just the "miracle" that had people going.

"See," he said, "showing off, well that won't get anyone anywhere. All it does is make people follow that person around and worship him. That's exactly the opposite direction from where you need to look. Going outside and making a parade behind another person will never, ever take you home."

"But Jesus did some of that." I thought silently, please don't start challenging what Jesus did. That's the one thing that hasn't been touched today.

"Actually, he didn't." Daniel said quietly.

"What?" Somewhere along the line, I had started to shake.

"Just a good marketing campaign." The little boy replied. As I stared after him in astonishment, he walked away, his small body disappearing into the diffused silver light.

Chapter 29

"Wait! Please, wait!" I ran after him in desperation, rapidly finding myself lost in an ultraviolet fog. There it was, that sensation of my mind falling to one side; I would not be surprised if it finally found its way through my ear and onto the ground. In fact, it was quite amazing I had any brain left at this point, yet there it was, on an inexorable journey far outside my control.

"Daniel, where are you? For God's sake, don't leave me with that!" I looked frantically around me, unable to see anything at all. Then it occurred to me, "O.K. I'm in the middle of my own soul. I don't have to panic. I don't have to build myself a capsule, just because I'm afraid." I took in a deep breath and felt an immediate calming sensation flow like warm honey through my body. "I'm perfectly all right. If I stayed here forever, I would be absolutely all right."

"That's so good, Rick!" Daniel seemed to take form immediately in front of me. Holding an ice cream cone, he licked some of the dark, rich chocolate from his thumb.

"How do you do that?" I was momentarily distracted by his ability to simply materialize. He had an ice cream cone. We were standing in the middle of my very soul and he had ice cream! I steadied my mind and aimed it toward more important things. "Wait, never mind, I want to know what you meant back there! When you said Jesus didn't do the miracles and it was just a marketing thing."

Taking an enormous bite, he casually offered, "Just confused stories which people starting using so they could have more power. My goodness, what's been written in your Bible is an awful mess."

I spoke very slowly to buy myself some time, "What are you saying?"

"Well, did you ever actually read what you call the New Testament?"

I quickly answered, "Sure. . . of course I have." Seeing he knew I wasn't telling the complete truth I added, "I can't say I could tell you exactly what's in it."

"See! That's part of the problem. You think you know what's there, but you don't even read it. If you did, maybe some lights would go on! They have Jesus saying really terrible stuff about punishment and going to eternal damnation and how you have to follow a God who acts like he hates all of you. . . things like that."

"That does sound familiar."

"You guys leave everything up to the keepers and never really look at it for yourselves. If you took the time to examine that document, you'd see how really cruel it sounds. How could that be right?"

Instinctively, I felt I should defend the most hallowed work of our civilization. "But isn't there a lot about how we can all be saved from all of that if we follow Jesus? Isn't that what he came to do, save us all from death. . . and the punishment we deserve because of the way we behave?" Wait a minute, we had already talked about this. Why would a loving God send his son to die so that he wouldn't kill us all?

"Nope," he said, taking the last bite of the sugar cone.

"Why did he come, then?"

Drawing a forearm across his mouth to wipe the chocolate away, he answered, "To teach everybody the same things I've been trying to tell you about."

I felt light headed, "Daniel, are you telling me that the words of Jesus. . . even the miracles ascribed to Jesus aren't true?"

"Yep."

That thunderbolt was out there somewhere; I knew it in my bones. Voice trembling I said, "Maybe you'd better tell me what he did say and do."

"He came to teach you about density, and the capsule and social mind and the soul which surrounds you. Like I said, just what I've been trying to tell you about. It's not that he didn't help people heal their bodies, of course he did, but not through miracles." Surveying the dazed expression on my face he said, "Maybe I better tell you about how it all got so mixed up."

"That would be good," I said shakily.

"Two things, density and power."

"O.K." That seemed like the least dangerous response I could generate.

154

"See, lots of people who were there didn't understand what Jesus was saying in the first place. That's what happens when we try to teach you guys. If you're locked into density and only rely on your senses, then that's how you experience and understand everything." He shrugged his small shoulders and looked at me as if I would have something intelligent to add.

"O.K." Again, safety seemed the best option, and I looked at him with the same expectation.

He did me the favor of continuing his explanation, "So, Jesus talked and did a lot and some people were able to understand it and some weren't."

"Because some were more trapped in density than others?" Good. I was actually all right, so far. I understood what he was saying and it wasn't that bad.

The little boy took it a step further, "Yep. See, all that stuff about coming to die for your sins so you could be forever saved in the kingdom of heaven. . . well, that's not what he said at all."

"What did he say?" I decided to go for it. After all, I had to know as much as I could if I was going to stay out of that capsule.

"It was all about density," he answered. "If you don't choose to set it down, well then you have to live all alone in your capsule and you never experience the joy and love that surrounds you. That's what he meant by the kingdom of heaven. It's right here! It's with you all the time. You're the one who locks himself up in a little dark room. Your soul doesn't move away from you. And if you live all separated like that, you're going to be awfully scared about death. That's why the story about the resurrection got started."

"The story. . ." Bravery leaked out the soles of my feet at the prospect of what he might say next.

"Yep," he nodded. "See, Jesus did come in a body, just like all human beings do. And, the people with lots of really horrible density killed that body. But the body didn't come back. Why in the world would that be necessary! Who wants to stay in their little container?" Clearly, Daniel thought it was an awful idea.

The lessons of my childhood church would not give way easily. "The resurrection. . . he rose on the third day. . . that's not true?"

"Well kind of, sort of, not exactly. . . " He gazed off in the distance for a moment and then said, "See, all along he kept trying to tell people all about who they really were, just like I've been trying to tell you. Finally,

Jesus said, 'O.K., all right, tell you what. . . these people around here are getting pretty upset with what I've been saying. So, I'm going to just hang out and let it come to its inevitable dense end. I bet they'll kill me. And then, I'll show you what I've been saying all along is true. People, you are not your body! You do not end when it does! Furthermore, you can connect with your own timeless, immortal self while you are still in your body if you stop being so addicted to social mind and get on with the work you have to do!' That's what he said. And guess what happened?"

"Some of them got it and a lot didn't." All right, that was easy to see. After all, even in a simple classroom situation, there are always people who don't understand the material, no matter how great a teacher you think you are.

"Yep. And know what else?" He said, raising his arms out to his sides and letting them fall back again.

"No."

"That worked out really well for people with active social minds who were standing around wanting to grab some of the fame and power that they thought Jesus had."

"What do you mean?"

"Well," he said, sounding a little exasperated, "people are so scared about death, they figured they could just make the resurrection thing literal. . . you know, everybody would be really impressed if his actual physical body showed up again, not just some spirit kind of thing. But, they decided if they were the ones who actually saw the live, dead body walking around and the other people didn't, well. . . ."

Forcefully, I responded, "They would be important. . . people would feel their only connection with that miracle was through the ones who were right there to see it."

"Bingo! That's the right word, isn't it?" He muttered to himself, "That's the strangest word."

Sometimes his ability to divert from the subject at hand was maddening. "Yes it is, Daniel, please go on."

"Well, next thing you know, the ones who claimed to see the actual body said they were the only ones that people should follow around from then on. And once they died, the people who had followed them around said they should have the power and everybody should only follow them around and there you go. . . the Catholic church."

"What?" I had never been a part of the Catholic church, but I knew enough about it to be sure you shouldn't take it lightly. After all, it had been around for 2,000 years.

"Yep. Invincible pope, bishops, priests and deacons. They have the truth, because they knew somebody who knew somebody who knew somebody who actually saw the body after it was dead walking around. Catholic, that word just means universal. In other words, they're in charge, there can be only one way of looking at this because they have the truth, period, and that's all there is to it. And furthermore, if you don't follow them, they won't tell you what that truth is and then. . ."

"God will punish you and you'll end up in hell." The deception of the ages was beginning to dawn on me. "But the whole time, the body itself did not rise from the dead?"

"No. But who cares?" he said, shocking me with his ability to overturn cherished beliefs with a single phrase. "That's not in the least bit important. Isn't it a whole lot more important to understand that you are more than your body right this very second! Not when it dies, not later when you get saved by somebody, but right now!"

My poor battered mind took a last stab at protecting itself, "You're reinterpreting the Bible, for God's sake!"

"Well, no, actually I'm explaining an important part of the Bible for man's sake." He looked at me innocently and continued on. "Jesus was one of the greatest teachers human beings ever had. Don't you think it's important for people to understand what he actually said? Why should the people of Earth be left to try to live by something so mixed up all it creates is pain and more time being lost? That's what he came to save you from, being lost!"

"Save us from being lost?" I gulped hard and said, "That certainly doesn't have the same punch as being crucified to save us from death and the punishment of an angry God, does it?"

The child raised his hands high in the air and yelled, "That's what I mean, that's how it happened! You know what else? It's not even consistent. Do you know who the very first person was to see Jesus after his physical body was destroyed?"

"No. I guess I should have paid more attention in Sunday school."

Eyes shining with excitement at being able to set things straight again, he explained, "Well, it was someone who had listened carefully the whole time Jesus was trying to teach people. It was someone who did not lie about seeing him walk around in a physical body after it was crucified. It was someone who had learned how to see beyond physical reality and so was able to clearly see Jesus even after his body was gone."

"Who, Daniel? Tell me, who was it?"

He smiled, "It was a woman. . . do you think they included her when they said people should only follow those who actually saw him?"

"Probably not." After all, even in today's world, we had a hard time giving women credit for anything.

He shrugged his shoulders and continued, "No, they didn't. Instead, they lied and said they had seen an actual, physical resurrection from the dead. They didn't see that because it didn't happen! They dismissed her perceptions as imaginary, just like you guys ignore what you can't see with your eyes."

"Are you saying the whole physical resurrection story was a lie, something made up by a whole bunch of people who only wanted power!"

"Yep."

"But, there was someone who saw Jesus, not in his 'risen from the dead' physical body, but beyond that body? Somebody who had learned from him about how to see beyond what can be seen with the eyes?"

"Yep. Yet even to this day, the Catholic church tells people to follow the succession of authority which is based on those who actually saw the physical body moving around after it was crucified. But doesn't allow women into the priesthood, even though a woman was the first one to honestly and truly see him. Know why?"

I gave it a try, "Prevailing sexist attitudes?"

"In a way," he nodded. "But it's worse than that."

My stomach began to sound a familiar alert, "What do you mean?"

He charged ahead, "Well, that's where the masculine way of seeing things took over most of the world."

"What?" I said, feeling like I had started down the steep side of the roller coaster.

Showing no mercy, he went on, "Yep. See God was established in your Old Testament as masculine. But Jesus shook all of that up right away. He made it perfectly clear that it did not matter at all whether your soul created a female or a male body. Boy, the guys who wanted power did not want that out there at all. The last thing they could afford was to have the Son of God run around telling everybody women were equal. You guys are just getting around to that concept in America in the 20th century!"

Receiving only a dazed expression as a response, he continued, "Anyway, a woman was one of the people who really understood what Jesus was really talking about. Want to know why?"

"Of course I want to know why. . . " I answered weakly.

"Because she used feminine ways of knowing things to hear what Jesus meant when he taught."

"So, Jesus teachings were more in line with feminine abilities? But, Daniel, what about all of the men? Didn't he come to help us too?"

"Oh Rick, do you think you are only male just because your body happens to be male? All of this division between male people and female people. Really, all of you are both. . . I mean, you all have complete ways of knowing and understanding things inside, but then you look down at your body and decide what to throw out depending on what parts you have. That's pretty dumb, don't you think?" His eyes were wide with amazement that we chose to mutilate ourselves in that way.

"Well," I replied, "when you put it that way, it is a ridiculous idea."

"Yep. See, the rightful leader of the church, if there was going to be a church, wasn't Peter at all. He was only one of the people who misunderstood what Jesus said. He took everything very literally and by doing that, he missed the whole point."

The sensibilities I had left began to wave a white flag, "Are you saying what I think you are?

"Yep," he said as he went straight for the knees, "The rightful leader was that woman I was talking about. The rightful leader was Mary Magdalen."

My defenses crumpled to the floor and I breathed, "Daniel, my God, Daniel, the former prostitute?"

"Lover of Jesus. . . body, mind and spirit." He said simply, shattering what was left of my concept of Jesus.

I managed to squeak out, "Oh God."

"Well of course he had a lover. He had a grownup man body. Why wouldn't he want to be loved in that way?" This point seemed perfectly obvious to Daniel, but it was directly contrary to everything we had been taught and I felt sick.

"I need to sit down," I said, finding myself already cross-legged on the field of light. It was so lovely here, sparkling drifts of pink and violet light made their way over me like dandelion dust on a summer's day. I brought my mind back to hear Daniel continuing with the story.

"So anyway, she should have been the leader, not because she was so close to him, but because she truly understood what he was saying. But they wouldn't let her. Most of them only heard with the masculine mind and they made everything Jesus said absolutely literal. All that beautiful poetry, that wonderful way of explaining things to people who were very, very lost. . . it all was understood to be literal.

"Not only that," he added, "by not wanting to hear Jesus when he talked about the equality between men and women, they reinforced the masculine concept of God. God continued to be this big, awful father in the sky thing, patriarchal, punishing, law dispensing. . . you know, justice, vengeance, power over other people. . . male stuff, the kind of stuff that has to be reckoned with by the same kinds of energies. That made it so the only right way to deal with anything was through the rational, sense-based mind. And right out the window went all the feminine elements. . . intuition, feelings, listening to the inner voice, inductive reasoning."

"Let me see if I understand this," I said, looking up at the little boy. "You're saying we made the masculine viewpoint a god and proceeded to worship both the figure we created and that way of looking at reality. Meanwhile, what we needed to do was include both ways, masculine and feminine?"

"Yep. See, the masculine energy provided the organizational abilities that it took to get the Christian message out all over the world. It provided the kind of focused drive that it took to make sure that nobody gave up, that they kept going until everyone heard what they had to say. The masculine energy did the recording, the ordering of information, making sure people got that information. The only problem was, it was incorrect information. They had it all mixed up, because they didn't hear it right in the first place!"

As if it could help me somehow, I shook my head and said, "I need to make sure you're not talking about men and women here."

"No. I'm not saying it was the fault of men. I'm saying you guys decided only a certain kind of energy was acceptable and then you threw out the part that would have allowed you to understand Jesus in the first place. And since you didn't understand what he said, the message got all confused and solidified into a masculine energy church with male people in charge of it."

I could hardly believe we hadn't seen these things for ourselves. "And then we used those directions in the mixed up Bible, like you were telling me before, to form our communities, our nations, our relationships with each other."

"Yep," he said and stopped, grief filling his eyes. "And you guys used those misunderstandings, and the unbalanced masculine energy to run all over the Earth killing people and demanding they believe the same thing as you do."

The Crusades, the Inquisition, the destruction of native cultures across the globe, much of it had been in the name of the church. Furthermore, we were attacking our very home. "Wait a minute! If we exclude the feminine, we're excluding Gaia!"

"Yep. That's why you treat her the way you do. That kind of horrible disrespect, that's the way you treat all that's feminine. . . run over it, control it, abuse it, don't listen to it, take from it without concern about how it's going to be afterwards."

"That sounds like feminist politics. . ." I said warily.

"No. . . actually, I hate to say this, but feminist politics is really just more worship of masculine energies."

"What?"

"Yep," he nodded. "It's just saying that those energies should be applied to and used by people in female bodies as much as by people in male bodies. They don't like feminine energy any better than anyone else."

Mulling that over for a second, something else occurred to me. "Daniel, this has something to do with why we are so homophobic, doesn't it? Gay people are tremendously persecuted."

"Yep. You hate the female energy you see in gay people, and you hate the male energy you see coming from lesbian people. You only feel safe if male energy comes out of male people and female energy comes out of female people. That way, you can identify it easier and be sure the female energy stays under control. But like I said, you all really have both kinds of energies."

I took a deep breath and brought us back to the point, "Tell me some more of what Jesus really said. . ."

161

"O.K.," he answered agreeably. "Well let's see, first of all, your Bible and your keepers insist on telling people that God is way, way out there somewhere. And you guys are all these little, pitiful things that are going to be squashed one day if you don't shape up."

"Jesus didn't agree?"

He grinned at me and said, "Of course not, silly! You're divine energy. The energy of the all flows continuously through your soul. The only thing that makes you pitiful and small is your own social mind and your dedication to the worship of it and creating a capsule and then mucking it all up with density."

My courage was rising. "And this issue of needing to be saved?"

"Well, you do need that, but not in the way people have been led to believe." His eyes searched mine and then he continued, "You do need to be saved from your misunderstanding and your desperate attempts to protect yourselves by building walls of density. And, we keep trying to save you by giving you all the information you need, by giving visionary experiences, providing the encouragement, sending our love, but you have to decide to dismantle your own capsule and your own social mind. You created it, it's yours to maintain or destroy."

"So, what about this idea that we're sinful and Jesus wants us to repent and accept salvation?"

He shrugged his shoulders and replied, "Well, its all garbled up. Remember, sin means to be apart from God, or apart from your soul. So, the mechanisms which allow for that are density and social mind. You punish yourselves by remaining apart from everything which can sustain you."

I was on a roll now, "Salvation?"

"That means to rejoin. . . " He stopped, face full of love and his voice overflowing with kindness, "Rejoin your soul, be as a little child in the arms of one who loves you so passionately, so deeply, so completely you could never want for anything again. "

That heavy, frightening word, "salvation," the one which had tormented us for hundreds of years, all it meant was to come home! I had to ask, "Jesus actually talked about that? About rejoining?"

"Well sure!" Daniel exclaimed. "His words were all about learning that social mind exists. When it walls itself off from your soul, it makes those little kingdoms of illusion and catches you in those illusions. Then you're really, really lost, because the more you get caught, the less you can see

162

your soul. Once you're are all alone, you panic. Then, it's really got you because the way out requires opening up your heart, not constricting with fear."

I took a deep breath, "Are you trying to tell me that Jesus was some kind of guide. . . a teacher who simply wanted to tell us how we could melt our capsule and have a reunion with the soul?"

"Yep," he replied, again watching shock waves pass through me. "Know what? One thing Jesus kept telling them over and over again was 'I am not your master.' Boy, did that ever get mixed up!"

"Wait a minute, church people are always saying you have to make Jesus your Lord and Master!"

"I know," he said sadly. "That's pretty terrible because it makes you look outside and inside is where it all is. See Jesus told them that! He said, 'I can show you guys how to do it, I'll tell you, I'll even light the way with my own soul energies through this body, but you have to do it yourselves. Don't follow me around and hope I'll take care of it for you. I can't. Wouldn't be right at all'."

"Why did they record it in the opposite way? The way I've heard it, Jesus tells them they have to follow him or it's all over, over now and over in eternity!"

"I know, Rick. Think how frustrating it is for us to see it all end up like that! If someone is your master, you don't have to think for yourself. You simply do what they tell you. And, if that master is gone, you do what his successors tell you to do. And then, they have you. You're just a worker bee, cut off from his own freedom, his own abilities, his own capacity to be what he was meant to be in the first place."

"Daniel," I said climbing to my feet, "are you saying our whole religious tradition is just the politics of power?"

"Well, not all of it, but most of it. That's what happens when people just try to find a leader and follow him around. Reconnection with your soul is something you have to do. We can help. We have always tried to help you, but you have to do it."

"He didn't want people relying on him?"

"Jesus tried to prevent all of that, you know all the worshiping and following, but even that was misunderstood. It's recorded as him being unwilling to stand up and say clearly who he was. He just wanted you to all learn how to have access to your own spiritual life, your own understanding and more importantly, your own experience."

He waited for my knees to quit shaking and then continued, "See, the purpose of a spiritual teacher is to help you until you learn to rejoin with your own soul. Then he should say goodbye. You won't need him any more. You're supposed to outgrow him. Jesus wasn't your master. If you had to keep being dependent forever and ever on him telling you what to do, that would really mean he was an awful teacher."

"That makes sense," I said sadly. "It sure is contrary to what we've been told."

He nodded. "Once you know your own soul, you're the same as Jesus. You know who you really are and he did, too. See, that resurrection story wasn't somebody's weird fantasy. It's an important story, but it's about getting out of the dead world of your capsule. Captured in walls of density, with no connection to love and beauty. . . that is death. I guess you could say that life the way most of you live it is death, and death is life."

I shivered, remembering the sight of myself desperately trying to get out of that prison. "You mean living in the capsule, it's cut off, density filled, suffocating."

"Yep. By showing himself after they stopped his body, he was just showing you the reality of what truly exists, who you really are and how to get there so you could be free and alive again."

I found a little smile and asked, "So, it's really more similar to the teachings of the East. . . the ones about the illusion of the world and the need for enlightenment, just like the masters of the East?"

To my surprise, he wrinkled his face in distaste and said, "Well, people mixed those teachings up in an awful way. You can't rely on them either."

"We can't? Those are garbled, too?" Despite my questioning, what he had told me made perfect sense. People following the Koran, the Talmud and other religious teachings weren't doing any better than we were. They had the same problems: violence, poverty, anxiety, alienation.

The little boy interrupted my thoughts, "But, who do you think the masters of the East were?" He watched me, blue eyes sparkling with anticipation.

"I have no idea."

"Of course you do, Rick!" He began to laugh and twirled around, arms outstretched, lifting his head upwards, as if to the sun. "It's all us! It's always been us!"

The light field began to shift and change, like an ocean suddenly enlivened by a storm. Great waves of light swept back and forth, beauty beyond human experience. Ultraviolet blue, pink, yellow, silver and gold, the enormous sea began to find form.

As if heaven itself had unfastened and opened, a great light appeared, golden rays streamed toward me and I shielded my eyes by instinct. But I did not need to, for this was the light of purest love. Still, I was afraid, until I saw in that light a luminous presence, moving, shifting its boundaries, now almost clear, now almost gone, a child, a glorious child, light pouring from her heart, shooting from her eyes and in her hands, the Earth.

And as I watched awe-struck, she became a man and his hands held all the stars and with immense joy, he scattered them outwards and they became planets, spinning in the darkness. And he became a boy child and held the wooden cross, bloody and worn, and I knew for the first time what it meant. The horizontal arms were our life on the Earth, the vertical our journey from density home again to our soul. And the child smiled and drew with a spectacular blue light a circle around the middle and I knew at last, that circle was my heart, the meeting place forever of Earthtime and the heavens.

And the child walked toward me and shifted form a thousand times as he approached, now the Jesus of my childhood, now the Buddha I had learned of as I grew, and now all the other teachers of Earth in both male and female bodies. In magnificent harmony, black, white, red, brown and yellow, they moved in and out of one another with no hesitation. It was so clear, they were all one teacher. There had never been any change in the message we were given. There was no confusion, except that which we had brought with us when we tried to hear. The message did not need to be different because it was ultimately so simple.

"Please come home, do not live alone and in pain. You are loved beyond all you can imagine. And we long for each of you and wait for you as the son and daughter lost long ago. We surround you forever and ever, wishing with a mighty heart for you to open the door of the prison you have made and at last. . . at last, come home."

I fell to my knees and sobbed, reaching out my arms to this woman-man-child who loved me so much and the luminous presence became a spinning sphere, shimmering, whirling red and silver light and coming toward me, entered my heart and exploded ecstatically and I heard without sound, "Never be afraid, I am with you always. . ."

Chapter 30

The infinite heart turns, quiet and full, and you are contained forever in that heart. And turn your own heart as we have shown you; turn in harmony with that infinite one. Come all hearts across your world, turn in love with Gaia, being from heaven whose love is strong enough to help you find your way home.

She waits as all the beings of heaven wait, for you to choose. And each action is noticed and there is great celebration for each choice you make which leads you home. Never think you are not longed for. Never think the arms do not wait. Never think the infinite heart does not know where you are.

My hands had been taken by the boy child and he led me into the great light and I held no fear of going. The boundaries of my being melted and I was as one with him. It no longer mattered who I had been; I was going home. Forever they had waited for me with a patience beyond that of all mankind put together. And now, it was time for me to return home.

I went, body shattering into a million particles of light, only a heart left, only a heart held by two small hands. And the cross had dissolved, leaving behind only the blue circle which now surrounded me. And my light danced with all that around me, endlessly moving, mighty heart beating forever and ever as one. And "Rick," Rick the capsule man was gone and was no more and it did not matter. I was going home.

And the boy child smiled as wide as the universe and my heart looked from its position in his hands upwards into his face and knew at last why he had come.

"We get another chance, don't we?" With no voice, my heart had dared to ask the unthinkable, and the boy child's love cascaded over me and I entered a new realm of ecstasy with the confirmation that there was more than enough love to offer mankind another chance.

"What can I do? What do you wish from me?"

And my heart looked to find the Earth in the same hands. I could hear Earth's people calling desperately for the help of the angry god and I saw their pain and panic could lead them nowhere, even as mine had never done.

"What do you wish from me?"

We walked into the spellbinding light and from there I could see the Earth's people, caught in their capsules, struggling in agony and fear. But, here and there, I could see a heart wheel turning, clogged and filled with debris, but turning. And where there was such a heart, soul light came into the world. And where there was soul light, Gaia's creatures were healthy and green and all the people around such a heart were awakened and beginning to stumble on their own journey to freedom.

"What can I do?"

And suddenly I knew I was going into the realm of heaven and I did not know if that meant I would never recreate my body again, but I did not care. And through the beams of silver, gold, pink and violet light we traveled, my heart, the center of all that I was, still held in the hands of the boy child. And I looked out across the light to the edge where I could see darkness and in that darkness, a collection of souls looked outward and cried for home. And I saw them, beautiful, shimmering, translucent, incandescent beauty itself, lost together looking for the unity of long ago, the home from which they had become lost.

"What do you wish from me?"

My heart swelled and wept for the tragedy of it all. For the misunderstanding, the fear, the anguish, the suffering on the Earth and in this place of the lost souls. And I knew at once, the only way home was through the heart of Gaia. That was why she had come. My heart's tears transformed into shooting beams of silver light and I watched them skip over the hands of the boy child and out into forever.

"What can I do?"

And I saw there was only one way for Earth's people to find home. We must find a strength, a desire which could send up a tremendous cry for freedom as deep and as powerful as anything we had ever known before. We must throw off the mantle of ignorance and refuse to remain separated from the truth of our being.

I knew we must look within and never stop until we had gone so far within that we were past the capsule. It was not enough to be self-consumed with concerns of the capsule, as our physicians and counselors had taught us to be. "Within" did not mean apart from the world, selfish and self absorbed. It meant true destruction of what we had thought of as self. The social mind had to be starved into extinction. We could no longer feed it, but must find a way to send it away forever.

And we went forward together and I watched the luminous path clear wide, and beckoning energy filled my heart. It grew and grew until I was standing again on my own. Still, all that remained of me was my heart, now able to direct itself to service sustained by love.

I stood ready to receive my instruction, knowing the ultimate stage of my growth could only be service to humanity. I could only do this in freedom from my capsule. I could only do this by bringing my soul's energies straight into the Earthtime.

And we walked farther into the calling and the longing and the love and it strengthened me and sustained me as I went, I had no need to look back to the past to what I had been. It had blown away, as inconsequential as dust on a towering tree.

Pure love awaited me and awakened me further and I remembered! At once, I remembered!

The infinite heart is filled with the love which animates all things. Know from that mighty place of love is sent forth the breath which makes life in all things. And so, love is the first force and life is the second. And as you exist on your Earth, know that each breath is propelled by love. And while you are on Earth, notice between each breath, there is a small silence. Know in that silence is infinite love which goes nowhere and is never empty. You may draw forth that love with your inhalation and send that breath of life back as a gift to the mighty heart as you exhale. In this way, there is a sacred circle, repeated hundreds of times in each of your days upon the Earth.

You see your lifetimes are only circles, drawing forth a vehicle to use in your journey to transformation and returning that vehicle when you are through. It is always, and will forever be, but only a drawing forth from the silence of love which animates all things and a giving back, even as your breath is pulled in, used and given back.

Ahead of me, pure glory unbound, unfettered, sparkling freedom, well-spring of love, I found myself again. I saw how I spun this lifetime called

"Rick." I brought Adam into being and sent him out to create my vehicle, my body and, in absolute love for me, he had done so well. And I saw my second spirit, bringing forth my consciousness of self, my "I am alive" awareness.

My soul looked at me and welcomed me and took my heart's hands in his and hers and whispered to me, "Welcome my sweet child, my creation, my beautiful daughter-son, welcome home, welcome back to the heart of all hearts. You have done well. Thank you for your service to my evolution. Thank you for your willingness to hear me, to move in ways that I asked. I bless your existence in the Earthtime.

"Your life has not rushed inexorably toward death, but your soul has ever moved toward you. Without interruption, I have whispered to you. In the silence of night, in the emptiness of life's pain, I have quietly sustained you.

"I am yours, a lover whose destination is the center of your heart. Thought forever gone, the union is again before you. Watch as glorious waves of joy and love encompass you as all souls sing and everywhere, hearts lift as one lost finds home again.

"What is real can never be truly lost and all that is not real can do nothing in its presence but fall away. See my eyes filled with unbearable compassion, unsurpassable love, glorious purpose, coming to meet only with yours. There is no reason to fear, for you see, nothing, no thing is unforgivable in the eyes of the soul.

"Come now. . . come straight into the embrace which has waited for you alone. Come into this sacred place and know me. Infuse your life with the light of its rightful owner. And as light fuses once again with light, only then will you find peace forever." My heart exploded into infinite showers of love and transformed again; I knew I would see more.

We arrived in the place where all lifetimes are born. A gentle wind wafted across a great plain and I saw millions of sparkling souls gathered together in loving groups. And as I watched, the souls spun gold and silver light and created Adams and second spirits. They poured love through each strand and breathed a soft breath into each one. The first and second spirits would go into the Earthtime, extensions of the third spirit. I understood that each soul belonged to a community, not of place but of purpose. Membership in a particular community was designed to further that soul's evolution.

In the midst of the gracious love of each community, individual souls carefully created an intricate pattern, an incandescent, glorious matrix born of that soul's purpose. Like morning dew caught on a complex spider's web, glowing particles of light clung to each pattern. Within those particles, information was stored so that the first spirit could know how to construct the body on the Earth. Dancing inside each particle was intimate knowledge about the soul's community so that the second spirit could follow its rightful path during a lifetime.

There was such beauty and purpose in this place, for everything was in service to the soul's evolution. And they sent those first and second spirits into the Earthtime together with their pattern in order to bring back the information necessary for the soul's advancement. And I heard the newborn cry of a thousand beings and saw in their eyes the reflection of the soul and heard their hearts call out, "Do not leave me here! Do not leave me in this little space! I want only to be with you, forever and ever." And I saw the spirits calm those hearts and silence the cries with gentle words, "Do not be afraid, I am with you always."

I drifted along on the shimmering wind, knowing for the first time that each person born into the Earthtime had at his or her core the information necessary for his successful journey. Only by acting in accordance with the intent of his soul could he truly find meaning and purpose in existence on Earth.

My heart went further and I heard unique music, traveling for all time, carrying the melodious message of each soul community.

"First Step" sang to me and I knew these souls spent their times on Earth helping others to find the first steps on the path homeward, their purpose service toward humanity's awakening. I saw them softly blow on the small fires in the hearts of men and women all across the Earth. And I saw them answering the first, tenuous questions that came when those hearts were no longer content to be the captives of social mind.

I saw them take a million hands and lead people back to the path that went toward home and once there, bid them a love-filled goodbye. Like rescuers in the black night on a stormy sea, they plucked people out of their unknowingness and set them on a course for shore. Then they would dive back into the density of Earth to find another voice calling out for help in the darkness.

As we walked further, I received a message from the "Healers." All across the Earthtime, they held hearts in their hands as the boy child had held mine. They spoke to Adams everywhere and gave him strength and courage to continue, even when social mind battered and betrayed him again and again. They mended the assaults density made to the connection to the third spirit and sent hope into the hearts of people everywhere.

Soon we passed by the "Community of the Line," theirs a warrior task in the lifetimes. For they drove back the darkness, keeping Earth and its beings safe from all that was not of the infinite heart. And they seemed never to grow tired, their purpose relying forever on an unwavering heart, an endless supply of courage and a knowingness that could discern what is from what seems to be.

And another soul group's music met my nonexistent ears and I knew they were of the "Consciousness of Christ." Their lifetimes were spent living, breathing and carrying the true message of his name's work. They were conduits for the truth of what a lifetime on Earth truly means and the reality of the soul which forever surrounds us. They wept for the destruction wrought on Earth in the name of Christ.

I heard, "Whenever two or more are called in my name, there I will be as well." And I understood the meaning for the first time. For wherever first and second spirit are spun forth, there the consciousness of pure spirit will be as well. I called to them and they answered with indescribable love.

We approached another assembled group and I heard terrible wailing and weeping and I knew without being told, these were "Gaia's people." They moved ever across the Earth, trying to protect her creatures, repair her skin, cleanse her body. And as they worked, density followed them like bitter black tar, encasing every living thing in suffocating sticky material. Still they worked, their hearts melting away the blackness wherever they could. And Gaia called them forth into the Earthtime in soul groups, knowing their work must be done in mass, the time long past when a single life could make a difference all on its own.

In the midst of the cries, I saw incredible beauty in the faces their Adams had created. They were the First People all across the Earth, brown, red, yellow, black and white. They rode the across the plains on pounding hoofs, ran through rainforests on powerful legs, nurtured forth her bounty and lived only for Gaia. And the drums called their warrior hearts forward, deep and resonant, ever willing to beat back the darkness of density, even as the war seemed lost.

Going on, I heard the "Community of Joseph." Quiet, willing companions for all those in service to humanity, strength and certainty of purpose radiated outwards from them. I knew they had been present in all times when Earth's people had moved forward in understanding the soul. And yet I knew they were seldom noticed, for theirs was a life of silent dedication.

This great place of light was filled with activity, spiritual purpose being formed and spun into the very fiber of the first and second spirits before they were sent into the Earthtime.

We went farther and found the returning place for those whose life on Earth was now over. And I knew clearly, the great love and powerful light which people reported seeing when they left their bodies at death was that of their own soul. The energy directed from the soul to sustain the vehicle condensed and a wondrous tunnel was formed. As the soul absorbed the information gathered by the personality during the lifetime, images of people it had known were released. Events of the lifetime were reviewed by the soul as the personality made its journey home into the astounding light. Immense, unwavering love poured out from the soul as once again, it welcomed its prodigal personality home.

I saw those souls drawing their first and second spirits back into themselves, gleaning experiences which were essential to each soul's own evolution. They greeted density battered hearts with love of an intensity never known inside the capsules of social mind. I watched multitudes of people drift upwards into the embrace of their souls and saw the relief, the jubilation as they finally knew the truth which had never changed. For there had never been any reason to fear death. This apparent tragedy was truly only a glorious reunion. With a burst of indescribable joy, love swept into limitless ecstasy, the personality disappeared into the light of the soul.

Before me, an immense pathway of translucent ultraviolet light appeared. My heart began to vibrate, resonating with a spectacular sound which seemed to be the song of forever. Dazzling fountains of blue and silver sparks flew outward in all directions and the intoxicating melody called me into itself. Drawn inexorably forward, I knew what I had thought was heaven had only been the beginning.

A place appeared before me where all souls were in glorious communion with one another. In one ecstatic dance of love, they spun together in service to all souls below them. This place was past any heaven I had ever dreamed of, and there was no angry God, no judge, no punishment.

The souls moved together and yet were still somehow apart. They looked deeply into the eyes of one another and found a well of love which never, never ended. Their work was powerful, for each one directed profound concern toward the souls in the region we had just left. Their endless love rained down on all the communities and strengthened them. They sang without ceasing, propelling those souls toward their own evolution.

From this place, some still created lifetimes upon the Earth. Whenever a particular soul's work was important for the care of Gaia or the advancement of consciousness, they would agree to accompany that soul for a while until it grew strong enough to go forth to fulfill its purpose alone. And then they bid goodbye and the energies went back into the lap of the soul so it could spin forth another lifetime, another escort for another being. For it seemed members of the second heaven had more than one vehicle on the Earth at once. Their energies were too powerful, their work too important to the evolution of all to wait for one life to return home.

My heart grew until it crossed the horizons of infinity and there I was surrounded with a blinding light from still another heaven. Endless waves of gossamer gold moved in all directions, seemingly propelled by a deep, steady throb which swallowed my being. Here, souls were no longer separated, but had become one boundless heart. Without ceasing, they gave glorious life to all the souls in the first and second heavens; by doing so, they gave life to all those on Earth.

The remaining solidified energy which kept my individual identity began to split and finally broke into a thousand shards of silver light which sent themselves out into forever. And then, there was no more separation, no more longing, no more understanding, nothing but love, an ecstatic, pure, powerful and enormous love.

And there in our arms, so tired, so afraid for her children, our sister Gaia was held. On splendid waves of golden light, she was nursed, ministered to, kept from dying. And the oceans were her blood, the rivers and streams her arteries, delivering nutrients throughout her body. And her hair, the magnificent trees blowing in the wind. . . her breath, the clouds in the sky.

And all around her, we sang our love and gave our encouragement. "Do not give up on them, our sister. Some are beginning to see. Perhaps soon, your burden will be lifted."

And she shuddered with grief and called to us, "Please help them to see. They do not know what they do."

And our waves of translucent gold rose and fell beneath her body and she sighed so softly and held her creatures to her breast. As she did, so many of them were too weak to drink and, no longer able to take her nourishment, they fell forever away. And her tears chased after them, out into infinity, an enormous sadness. . . a mother who can do nothing to save her children.

Here was the place from which humanity had fallen so long ago. All the souls of mankind were needed to make this heaven complete. We sent forth a deep yearning, and arms stretched out to all who remained below in the other heavens. The mighty heart cried for those who were lost, like a mother cries for her child in the darkness. For a million years, the cries had gone out.

Gaia had willingly left this place, and put herself into exile, ripped away from the body of the whole. She went to sustain those souls who were lost. She provided a way for them to return home. And still we created the undulating rhythm with Gaia in our arms, pushing love through her body, praying for mercy, offering hope. . . nourishment from upper heaven.

Even beyond this beyond the beyond place, there was something else. We could sense it there, infinite life breathing, infinite heart beating, forever and ever sending itself outward and bringing us back again. A voice called to us and that glorious sound sped along the strands of light which made our being, infusing us with rapture and a boundless determination. And Gaia's head lifted with joy and we knew there was a second chance for humanity, perhaps only one more opportunity before Gaia's body gave out.

And suddenly, I knew what was wished of me.

Chapter 31

It seemed I had been falling for a very long time. Wafting downwards on an invisible wind, I descended through the three heavens, past all those magnificent souls. Their eyes were everywhere, clear blue, like a perfect summer sky and radiating love and eternal compassion.

Born on the currents of love, my own soul joined with me and I watched it spin the body of "Rick" again, and my awareness of that person and his lifetime came fully back. I began to weep, knowing I must go back into the Earthtime and rejoin my destiny there. Again I heard, "Do not be afraid, I am with you always."

And like a comet goes across the night sky, light streamed from me in all directions and my heart reentered the body of "Rick," a tiny space, a small vehicle to live in for the next decades on Earth.

And Gaia reached up enormous arms and caught me, and I stopped falling, brought to her heart. And there was love surrounding me as powerful as all her seas. She would continue her agreement to sustain my life, and I had the responsibility to remember.

My soul spoke again, "Rick, you must remember all of this, for you must go forth into the Earthtime and help the others remember. That is the hope for all humanity, for each to remember who he really is."

The space grew tighter and tighter and my vision began to eclipse until I could only see with my physical eyes, like a creature caught in a box can only see through a crack in the seam.

"Do not identify with the body." I heard the voice of my soul. "You can continue to see and know, you do not have to obey your senses. Remember, Rick. You must remember."

At once I was not trapped any more, but continued to approach the surface of Earth with my ability to see beyond my senses, to know, to hear, to touch outside my little container.

There I was, suddenly standing again on firm ground, but it was no longer static and dead. I could feel Gaia breathing; I could hear her heart beating and mine in harmony with hers. I could see all the trees around me, the birds flying by, the bee which buzzed, they were all Gaia, different expressions of the same love. And when I looked at my surroundings, everything pulsed and hummed together, a living, breathing mosaic of love.

I moved my body slowly, again unfamiliar with my vehicle. Finding my own heart, I saw it turning rapidly, and light shot out all around me from that wheel. I knew I could never run out of that melodious energy, unless I forgot and clogged up its capacity to receive from its maker.

Light flowed from every surface of my body, a panoply of violet, pink, subtle orange and blue. And I smiled with delight when a passing butterfly felt welcome enough to land on my arm. I remembered, the little bug, the black, simple thing was my personality self, but the wings, the glorious wings, the colored expanse of beauty, that was my soul. And those wings vibrated softly and the colors shimmered and off she flew, carried high on a gentle wind.

I looked around me, trying to see where I might be on the Earth and recognized Idaho once again. And walking toward me the boy, Daniel. Kicking the dirt with his hightops like any other little kid, he grinned at me happily.

"Hi, Rick!" he said, as though nothing unusual had ever happened.

Looking at him with new eyes, I could see his heart wheel spinning with brilliant silver light. My own heart continued to expand, now with gratitude and the beginnings of either ecstasy or hysteria. Whatever it was, I had no hope of controlling it. I choked out a question for which I already had the answer. "Daniel, I did it, didn't I? It wasn't a dream. I was there, wasn't I?"

"Yep," he said with gentle appreciation of my accomplishment.

Falling over backwards can be a wonderful thing. It completely removes any pretense of being all right. You are free at that point to come completely unglued. I didn't really know what that meant, but I was tired of trying to prevent it. I was just going to lose it, fall apart, scream, cry, talk gibberish and be done with it. But nothing happened. I let go and nothing embarassing happened. To be sure, I was lying flat on my back, but it didn't seem to be particularly significant to anyone.

"Daniel?" I called out weakly. "Are you there?" Giant black basketballs floated in front of me, partially obscuring my vision.

Somewhere to my left, Daniel's voice sounded like it was under water. "Of course, where else would I be?"

"Don't leave me, O.K.?" I could not stand the thought of being alone.

"Okie dokey." The child's phrase lingered in my mind like an old melody, comforting somehow, familiar and warm.

Tears rained down my face and I dared to ask a single question, "Why me? Why did you show me?"

"Why not you?" he replied simply.

With a measure of embarrassment I responded, "Well, I guess I believe there are people who would be more worthy than I am. . . "

I was shocked when Daniel began laughing so hard he could scarcely breathe. Taking in an enormous gulp of air, he soon used it all up with another round of hysterical giggling. He managed to send out a few words, "Oh Rick! Do you try to be so silly or do you just do it naturally?"

"Wait a minute! What's so funny?" My feelings were hurt. After all, admitting there may be others in the world who are better people than you are is a difficult thing to do. The appropriate response should be a quiet and comforting, "of course you are as worthy as others, Rick." I certainly had not expected to be laughed at.

Nonetheless, the child continued to howl. "It's just after seeing everything, it seems so funny you would still think about who's better and who's not!"

I looked back at him with dismay and he suddenly stopped laughing and said, "For heaven's sake, Rick, that's what it's all about. . . getting over the idea that somebody else deserves to know more about spirit! We want all of you to see and know first hand, just like you were meant to. That's the whole point!"

He looked at me with a new compassion, "Don't you know by now that you are all so loved? You are all worthy of knowing the truth. Your soul waits to take you into its arms, it doesn't measure whether you deserve it or not. While you are busy feeling unworthy, it grieves for your suffering and constantly sings its love. But you see, your own bitter voice of condemnation drowns out that sweet sound."

178

The words softened what remained of my stubbornness and I began to cry again. He stood before me and reached out his hands and I took hold of them with the trust of a small child determined never to let go. Bringing my head to rest against his little chest, I heard him whisper, "Oh Rick, just remember who you really are."

And I closed my eyes and remembered it all. I knew now where I had come from and what I was surrounded by each and every day of my life. My soul was not "out there," or "up there," it was right here with me. It had been here all the time. It was me who turned my back on the boundless acceptance of my soul. I had never fallen short of being worthy to receive the love. It flowed constantly from my soul. Without judgment, it came consistently, endlessly, without interruption. It was me who blocked myself off from that wellspring. It had always been me.

And I knew I could no longer afford to allow myself to become lost. I had known first hand what only a few others had ever seen. I knew now what was possible for all human beings.

Quietly Daniel said, "See, this is a wonderful time for everybody. You all get a second chance."

Remembering that phrase, I opened my eyes and sat back. "Daniel, what does that mean? I know it's some kind of incredible opportunity for us, but I don't understand it."

The little boy plunked himself down on the grass and said, "Well, when the personality called Jesus came to your Earth, he started the time when the souls of the Christ Community would be at the center of helping you guys to remember. That time is about to end."

I said softly, "You know, I always thought there was one heaven and everybody would go there at death. At least that's what I thought when I believed in heaven at all." I hadn't really believed we would be wearing white robes and playing harps, which had always sounded like an awful waste of time. But I had thought there was only one place to go.

"Well," he said matter of factly, "there's more than one. And in the first heaven, souls are still spinning lifetimes so that they can gather information and experiences that will help their evolution." He busied himself by pulling blades of grass from the bottom of his shoe.

But I was riveted to our conversation, "Do you mean they're kind of climbing toward the higher heavens?"

"Yep. Wouldn't have to, except they all got so lost in the first place. Like I already told you." He gave up and pulled his shoe off and banged it on the ground, pounding away the remaining grass.

I had many friends who believed the soul was perfection itself and the only task was to grow enough to be able to consult that soul for our answers in life. But, if our soul was already entirely complete, why would we continue to need lifetimes? In the soul's need to evolve and our role in helping it to do so, for the first time I had an explanation that made sense!

"So, they're continuing to drop their density and regain the. . . the lightness, the purity to return all the way home?"

"Yep," he said, looking over at me.

With a new understanding of my life's purpose, I asked excitedly, "That's why it's so tremendously important that we remember who we are, isn't it? I mean, we need to do that so that we can liberate ourselves from social mind and help Gaia. But our souls rely on what we bring them in order to advance! What good are we to them if we're just thrashing around in the capsule?"

He smiled with pleasure as he watched me grasp the reality of my own true importance and replied, "Well, all experience is valuable. But you can certainly help a whole lot more if you're connected to what you're supposed to help. How else can you figure out about your life purpose?"

"Life purpose?" I had heard people talk about that many times. It seemed we were all searching for something which would help us make sense out of what we were doing on Earth. After all, life in the capsule didn't have anything at all to offer. Intuitively, we had always known that.

"Yep. See, most of you on the Earth belong to one of the communities. Of course, everything is always free will and you can do whatever you want to do. But your life will be a bunch more valuable and go a lot better if what you do is in agreement with your soul community." Somewhere along the line, he had taken off his other shoe and now tossed them casually aside.

I remembered watching as the souls actually wove their community affiliation into our very being on Earth. Excitedly I said, "I saw how the souls were spinning lifetimes using some kind of energy they got from their communities. That purpose is an integral part of who we are on Earth, isn't it?"

"Yep." He looked at me, knowing I had much more to ask.

"Daniel, this has tremendous implications! Everybody is always trying to figure out what they are doing on Earth, whether their life has any meaning, why they are here. By knowing how we should be in service to our soul, and knowing what community our soul comes from, that could answer an awful lot of questions." I took a very deep breath and felt immense relief inside. My whole life, I had been asking what the point of being here might be.

"Yep. See, when people try to do stuff apart from their soul, it never works out very well. There's a whole lot of people who are living in ways that have nothing to do with their deepest purpose. It makes for a lot of confusion and frustration and endless searching for meaning without ever finding it."

"I know. I know," I said passionately. "That's what most of my work as a counselor has been all about. I've tried really hard to help people find their true identity and meaning in life. But, I had no idea!"

He began to giggle, "I know about those funny tests your psychologists give people. You know, the ones that try to help them figure out what they should be doing!" He was laughing uproariously. "What a goofy thing to do!"

"Daniel, that's the best we had. None of us knew about communities or any of what I just saw!"

I thought about all the counselors I knew who really didn't have much feeling for helping people, and the doctors who were better at ordering supplies than they were at healing patients. I remembered policemen I had known who spent more time standing on the street corner trying to help some kid than they did running after criminals. Maybe these people had jobs that didn't match at all with their soul community!

I asked, "Did you say that the time of the Christ Community being in charge of people remembering is about to end?"

"Well, kind of sort of, not exactly. See, they were never in charge, they were just at the center for a while. But, you guys didn't respond very well, I must say that." He looked tremendously sad and added, "Do you know how many wars have been fought in the name of Jesus? The violence that people do to each other, both physically and emotionally while they argue about who is more dedicated to Jesus is terrible!"

"I know Daniel, and you showed me why. We had it all mixed up!"

181

He nodded. "It's been absolutely amazing to see you guys use what Christ had to say to increase the density on the Earth over the last two thousand years. That was pretty hard to do. . . I mean take something so beautiful and make it so dense." He paused and looked away before continuing, "But anyway, it's time for the Healing Community to come to the center of things."

"The Healing Community. . ." I thought for a moment and then saw them clearly in my mind. "Those are the souls I saw who seemed to soothe Adams and heal wounds, who were mediating difficulties between people, those who try to bring people together!"

"Yep." He gazed at me expectantly and then added, "But what's most important?"

I floundered for a moment and then remembered seeing something spectacular. "They were holding hearts in their hands! They were the only ones I saw doing that!"

"Yep." His eyes were bright with excitement.

My understanding was unfolding at a rapid pace. "So, Daniel, they must be at the center of helping people to awaken their hearts! Just like I've learned about mine! Are they going to help people unclog their heart wheels, so that the energies of the soul can find their way through the darkness we've created on Earth?"

"Yep." He looked at me intently, waiting for me to catch up with the importance of the shift into this very special community.

I could see the glorious possibilities. "Oh God, that could be a new beginning for Gaia, for all of Earth's people. If we can get our hearts moving again, everything could change!"

"Yep." A spectacular smile swept across his face as he replied.

Basking in the warmth of that smile, my enthusiasm suddenly was dampened with an additional realization. I looked over at the little boy and saw his smile fade as he understood what I was thinking. Quietly, I voiced my concern, "But social mind. . . social mind won't like that at all."

"No, it won't," he replied sadly.

"I can hear them now," I muttered in frustration. "Opening the heart is a ridiculous, sloppy, sentimental idea that doesn't have anything to do with reality."

He looked daunted himself. "That sounds about right."

I continued with a sarcastic tone, "And, then they'll say, 'We can't afford to do that, it's too dangerous in today's world to be running around opening ourselves up to who knows what.'"

"Yep." He looked with me with expectation. "And what would you answer, Rick?" The answer made its way up from my deepest being, "But you don't go outside into the world to do your work! It's all an inside job! It's not about cramming your philosophy down somebody's throat or spouting greeting card sentimentality. It's about you taking responsibility to clear away your own density and making your own heart wheel spin. That way, you can bring a new kind of energy into the world. . . not a concept about energy, not a philosophy about love, but an actual, tangible force that can change the world!"

He clapped his hands together and yelled, "That's so good, Rick!"

I was hyperventilating. "This second chance. . . will we have help, like when Jesus came? Will there be a new teacher to help us?" Surely if we were getting another chance, somebody was going to come and help us out.

"Yep," he said, his eyes looking serious again.

"Daniel, that's incredible! Wait a minute, is that what Jesus spoke of as the Second Coming?" With what I knew now, it couldn't be, but I wanted to ask anyway.

I was surprised at the vehemence with which he replied, "Boy, did that ever get mixed up!"

"Well, I can see that it must have been awfully confused." I had experienced the incredible beauty of the souls, I had received the astounding quality of love which was available for all of us. How could that be the result of some angry, punitive God?

I continued, "I mean, all that talk of an avenging God coming to get us and Jesus appearing and saving some people and not others while God destroys the Earth. What was that all about?"

"Just power and fear," he replied. "Jesus didn't say anything like that. All he was talking about was the fact that if you identify with your personality self and the little capsule, someday you will come to the end of your vehicle and it will look like the absolute end of your life. The body will be destroyed and everything you thought was important in your lifetime will be destroyed with it."

I thought for a moment and then said, "So, he was just saying that life is short. The 'end of the world is at hand' thing relates to us personally. We really don't last very long; we all die."

"Right. He was just trying to remind you guys about how to avoid that sense of a terrible end. Just learn to move your identity into the realm of the soul. It's right here; it is who you are and always will be. It never ends and it will always love you. It's you who walls yourself off from that. Don't stubbornly stay fixed inside the part which ends. Embrace yourself as something which exists forever."

"Wow. That did get mixed up! So, he was just teaching again about how our life on Earth does end. If we stay in the capsule and only know the body and the personality, death is a terribly scary thing to face. But if we come out of our capsule and know the whole time, first hand, who and what we are, then there is no end to be afraid of!"

"Yep. And, if you insist on identifying with your body, you may even try to stay with it after it's dead. Then, you will have more of the experiences talked about in Revelations."

I searched my memory, seeking to find details from the Bible's oddest book. "Isn't there stuff in there about dragons and monsters coming?"

"Yep." He thought for a moment and cryptically added, "Just bugs."

"Did you say bugs?" I had absolutely no idea what he might mean with that one.

"Yep. Well, they come after the body is dead, you know."

"Daniel, that's a horrible thought!" We were so phobic about death in America, we spent millions of dollars every year making sure the body would never decompose. Our embalming practices were just a manifestation of what he had been talking about. We were so terribly afraid that our body was who we are, we couldn't stand the idea of losing it, even at death!

The little boy broke into my thoughts and said, "The bugs are supposed to come. After all, the vehicle isn't of any value to you any more and they can use the materials for their lives. Anyway, if you are still there, not accepting that you aren't your body, well it can be an awful experience!"

I took in a deep breath and decided to go for it. "So, this idea of Jesus coming to save those who believe in him, all that was about was telling us again, believe in your own soul as represented by Jesus. Experience it, accept it and know that it is the only way out of the tragedy when your world ends. That's the only part which lives in heaven, so to speak, so that's the only way you will ever get there. I get it, Daniel! It's so simple! Be your soul and live forever, or be your personality and body and suffer horribly now, and at the end of your life."

"Yep," he said brightly. "It is pretty simple, don't you think?"

"Well, I do now!" It was tremendously simple. But like most of what I had learned today, it was nowhere near what I had been taught to believe. The funny thing about Revelations is nobody had known what to do with it. In my comparatively bland church tradition, Revelations was usually just ignored.

"Daniel, do you know how many scholars have tried to figure out what in the heck Revelations was all about!"

"Yep. Do you know how many keepers have terrified the people they were supposed to be helping? What a mess! No wonder your people fear God so much."

He looked at me sorrowfully and continued, "Pretty amazing to see what your keepers did with that. What you're reading now in the Bible took a long time to develop. They don't tell you that part."

I prepared myself for another book of the Bible to be rewritten before my eyes. "What do you mean?"

"Well," he said, "things were changed several times. Whenever they figured out what they needed to get more power, they just changed the stories all around. Not only did the message get scrambled in the first place, but my goodness, it's been changed a lot since then. If you ever want to study the myths of different places all around where the Bible was developed, you know ones from Greece and Rome and Persia, Egypt, Palestine. . . a lot of them are in Revelations."

"You mean Revelations is just a convenient collection of stories to scare people with?" I felt angry with yet another example of man's cruelty to his fellow man. For centuries, people had been terrified by the material in the last book of the Bible.

"Yep," he said, looking as though he would like to punch someone out.

I gathered myself back together and dared to ask another question, "Back to the help we're going to get. It won't be Jesus, will it?"

"No," he replied.

My stomach turned over in its familiar imitation of a tumbling match as I dared to ask, "Well, then who will it be?"

"You just have to watch for him." He looked at me as thought I would understand perfectly, but I did not.

"Watch for him? Will there be some kind of dramatic entrance? What should I look for?"

Exasperation powered his words, "Oh Rick, how do you think you will know?"

"I don't know. . . I have no idea. . ." I defended myself. How in the world was I supposed to guess that? But suddenly I was flooded with an amazing realization. I knew how I would know. Of course I would know! "Daniel, my heart! I'll know because I have a different heart now! I'll hear my soul tell me when the second chance begins!"

His face lit up and he cried, "That's so good, Rick!"

Excitement went through me like an electrical storm. "This opportunity will be seen by all of us who develop our hearts! The eyes and ears of the body will be irrelevant because this isn't something you see or hear. All those stories about trumpets and thunder, they aren't true at all!"

"Nope." He whispered dramatically, "Spirit is everywhere! But its energies are subtle. If you don't develop the capacity to perceive them, you'll never experience them. If you don't experience them, how would you know what's going on in that realm?"

I began whispering back before I realized mid-sentence there was no need to do so. "The help that's coming could be standing right in front of us and we wouldn't see it!"

"That's right," he shouted.

I felt incredibly invigorated about the possibilities ahead. "People have to start doing their work, Daniel! If they don't start unclogging and starting their wheels up again, they won't know when this wonderful help comes."

"Nope," he said, continuing with a scary thought, "if you don't have a way to receive the message, it won't matter how powerful the being is who sends it."

My God, while people were passively sitting waiting for a crack of lightening and the vengeful God to appear, our real help could be missed even if he was in our own front yard. I said excitedly, "Because Jesus didn't come to save us and this new teacher won't either. We have to do our own work. That's the bottom line, isn't it?"

He replied quietly, "Always has been, always will be."

"But we're never alone." It wasn't that we were abandoned and left adrift like some awful cosmic experiment, we were just stubbornly cutting ourselves off from what had surrounded us the whole time.

"Not unless you choose to be."

"But social mind is a terrible opponent. You said that, Daniel. It's the very opposite of spirit isn't it? All it wants to do is take all our natural power away, the power we gain from the energies of the soul. All it wants is to conquer and demolish spirit wherever it goes!" I could see how truly destructive this false part of ourselves was. It really wasn't just a simple critical voice within us, but a powerful force, actively opposed to the energies of spirit.

Passionately, I continued, "Social mind is what has always killed the wonderful teachers like Jesus who came to help us. And now it's attacking Gaia to the point that her body could give out entirely. All of us could be destroyed by something which takes everything subtle and beautiful, everything which is of the heart, and attacks it with a vengeance. . ." I trailed off as an incredible thought rose up like a tidal wave inside me. Looking at Daniel in amazement, I tried to bring up the courage with which to voice it.

For centuries, we had been warned of a terrible being who would come to Earth, spreading evil wherever he went. In the final days, this person would lead people toward their own destruction and fire would descend from the sky and kill all life on Earth, except those saved by Jesus. There were always rumors about who this person might be. The current speculation mentioned someone born in the Middle East. But what I was thinking was much more terrible than that. All this time, how could we have been so blind?

Taking a deep breath, I whispered, "That's it, isn't it? The terrible being we were told to watch out for, the evil one who attacks the soul and could actually destroy the world, I know who it is. My God, Daniel, I know who it is."

Chapter 32

The little child looked at me, confirming with his eyes that what I was thinking was actually true. Quietly, he encouraged me to bring it out into the open. "Go ahead, Rick. Go ahead and say it."

I squeaked out the horrible name, "The Antichrist." I gathered my courage, "It isn't an actual person who will come and lead an evil attack on humanity. It's worse than that." I gulped and continued, "The awful thing which is in the process of destroying us right now, it's not out there someplace. Daniel, it's right here, it's a part of us!"

Daniel looked soberly at me for a very long time and then said softly, "Yes it is, Rick." A tear washed down his cheek and he mournfully continued, "The Antichrist lives in all of you, because you create it, feed it and allow it. The time has come for you guys to decide, to make a real choice between the energies of soul or the energies of Social Mind. . . symbolized by Christ and the Antichrist.

Horrified, I choked out my next words, "And right now, the Antichrist is running rampant, isn't it? That's what's got us. If we don't stop it, the terrible stories will end up being true. We'll be devoured by ugliness, violence, and hatred for each other and the Earth."

"Yep," he replied.

My God, we had all been taught to watch out for this horrible thing. For hundreds of years, we had waited for this malevolent being to bring the world to an end. It had been more of the same, "search out there," behavior which had kept us lost for so long! While we were looking outside of ourselves for Jesus to save us from a terrible fate, all the while the energies of the soul and its destroyer had both been inside of us the whole time.

I wanted Daniel's confirmation of what I already knew was true, "This Antichrist, our own social mind, it's powerful and cunning, just like they always said, but it's inside of us! It isn't just some concept, it's real and it's destroying everything while we wait for something in the sky to come and save us!"

"Yep." Looking grief stricken, he continued on, "It's been social mind that waged the wars in the name of Christ. It's social mind that keeps you so separated from your heart that you can be horrendously violent to each other. It is social mind which looks at the color of someone's skin and then tells you they are fundamentally different from you. Social mind forms the opinions and makes the judgments which allow some of you to eat while others starve to death."

I would not allow myself to let his last statement go as irrelevant to my world and I cried, "Even in our own country, we have people living homeless on the streets! For God's sake, we have small children without anywhere to sleep!"

Daniel's face was strewn with tears as he added, "Social mind robs for energy. Then it convinces you it's all right to step over the bodies of those you judge morally unfit when they become too weak to make their way in the world."

Something appalling occurred to me. "Daniel, our churches. . . the way many of them function, aren't they just training centers for social mind?" Even at the most benign level, going to church was all about dressing up in your best clothes, putting the right amount of money in the collection plate, gossiping about what was going on with the other people there. But beyond that, it was starting to seem that there were much more dangerous things happening under the name of God.

I continued, "Several Protestant churches in Boise have outdoor sign boards. I saw one the other day that said, 'Love God, Point the Way to Salvation, Dispense Justice.' Dispense Justice! What in the world gives them the right to dispense justice?"

"Well," he replied, "all your other Christian churches came out of the Catholic Church. It was first and they all came later."

I searched my scrambled brain for information and then said, "Martin Luther in the Sixteenth Century . . . the Reformation and all of that."

"Right. That was supposed to liberate people from the hierarchical structure of the Catholic church. Through the right of succession, the priests

189

and bishops had always told people they had direct contact with God and it was only through them that anybody else could be heard. So, the Reformation was supposed to change all of that. . . anybody had the right to talk to God if they wanted to."

"O.K., I know all of that from a college class about comparative religion, but what's that got to do with justice?"

He took a deep breath and continued, "Well, before the Reformation, everybody was supposed to stay in line and be accountable to the church. After the Reformation, they were supposed to be directly accountable to God. But, people began to make other people accountable to them. You know, keep an eye on each other and 'straighten out the sinners' kind of a thing."

"So, you're saying instead of the priest having so much power because he had the only telephone connection to God, everybody was supposed to be able to do it themselves. When that happened, people started acting like priests and judging each other. Like when a parent leaves for a while and the kids start challenging each other for who's going to be in control."

"Right," he replied. "At least the Catholic church had some pretty clear standards about what it was going to judge somebody about. Once that misguided power went outward into the hands of everybody, well, lots of people starting feeling pretty righteous and behaving in ways that were pretty painful for other people."

It was starting to make sense to me, "And that got projected into an even bigger and more vengeful angry God in the sky."

"Yep. And everybody felt it was up to him or her to tell other people when they were being the right kind of person and when they weren't. And once they could do that, they could also tell people what horrible things God was going to do to them if they were bad. And that God out there kept getting bigger and more angry and mean all the time."

I had friends who came from churches with a terrifying concept of God. It seemed most of their time was spent quoting scripture and talking about the last days and how God was going to punish everybody. I couldn't take it and had quickly decided to avoid ever having a conversation about religion with them again. And yet, these frightening ideas seemed to permeate their discussions of even the most unrelated topics.

I came back to Daniel and asked, "They decided who should be punished on what basis?"

He replied, "Mixed up stuff from the Bible, mostly. But also, since it was all social mind deciding, it changed a lot, depending on what was going on with other social minds at the time. . . like what year it was, what part of the world it was."

I shook my head and said, "So, it just became a bunch of social minds interpreting an already mixed up Bible and beating each other up with it!"

He sighed and answered, "Yep. Sounds kind of funny until you realize what came of it."

I thought for a moment before saying, "So, dispensing justice means look at what your neighbor is doing and let him know when he's disobeying God as you understand it."

"Right," he nodded.

The headlines in my newspaper showed what that kind of thinking could lead to. "That can get pretty ugly, Daniel. We have people in our country who think it's justified to kill a doctor because of the kind of work he does."

"I know," he said sadly. "There's an awful lot of spiritual violence in your world."

I had never heard that term before. "Spiritual violence?"

"Yep. Emotional battering in the name of God. Ministers frightening the wits out of people with misunderstood stuff from the Bible. Telling them they are worthless sinners who are going to burn in hell forever unless they fall to their knees to the Lord and Master, Jesus Christ."

I remembered seeing another church sign, "What you decide to do with Jesus now will determine what he decides to do with you later. Repent while you can." It had been so horrible, I hadn't even understood what they meant for a few days.

The little boy continued on, "Pastors and parishioners telling people the blood of Jesus is on their hands unless they accept him as their Lord and Savior."

You could hear these kinds of statements at any time on Christian radio, not to mention the countless evangelical television shows and church services. "Daniel, this kind of thing is said a million times all over the Earth every day."

He looked at me for a moment and then said softly, "Social mind at work."

I was afraid to receive his reply to my next question, "Are you saying that the people who say this kind of thing are agents of the Antichrist?"

"Yep." He had a way of saying the most difficult things with a single word. I swallowed hard and listened. "By tearing people away from the soul which surrounds them through fear, intimidation, mixed up teaching and spiritual violence, they act as destroyers of spirit. They are in opposition to true spirit. They're just social minds stealing more power for themselves by scaring other people!"

I searched for a way out of my awful realization, "But you're not saying they are evil. . ."

He gazed at me without blinking, "Do you know what that word means, Rick?"

"No." I was surprised at myself. Evil was a word used all the time, but I really didn't know what it meant.

"Absence of light," he replied.

The three simple words simultaneously shocked me and caused every-thing to fall into place. It was all I could do to find my voice, "Oh God. . . it just means separated from the light of the soul, stuck in the darkness of the capsule which is formed by social mind. Evil just means that you are under the direction of social mind instead of spirit, doesn't it?"

"That's what it means," he answered, holding his hands out to his sides.

I found the courage to continue, "And anything which promotes judg-ment, fear, psychological battering, comparison and dependence on a wrathful deity could be considered evil because it separates you from your soul's light and keeps you locked in darkness. Oh my God."

"Yep. Just keeps you looking outward to the opinions and judgments of the minister, the church members and a far away, raging God."

There were so many churches and so many innocent people who wan-dered into them looking for comfort and a sense of hope. But, what really happened within those walls was awful. I sputtered, "And while you're distracted like that, social mind just grows and grows with energy and power like an engorged mosquito."

He looked at me soberly, "And the more separated you are from spirit, the more you can justify any kind of action against another person."

I knew exactly what he meant, "Like murder."

He nodded and replied, "Like murder, child beating, spouse abuse, racial violence."

My heart was pounding with the injustice of it all, and I said sarcastically, "This is done in the name of God. . . justified because the other person is not what you think they ought to be according to a horribly scrambled up mess of a message."

"That's how it works." His voice was filled with compassion.

I felt sick. "And it's all been a horrible, tragic misunderstanding."

Quietly he answered, "I'm afraid so."

How could we have gotten so far off track? What Jesus had come to say was so beautifully simple. I said softly, "The whole time, Jesus was really just trying to tell us how to clear our density, make our heart wheel turn with the energies of the soul. We were being instructed about how to offer another person those energies of love, just like we would want them to do for us."

He did not say anything, but I could see the grief in his eyes. We sat together for a long while, each filled with sadness at the tragedy of it all. Mankind had been given so many wonderful teachers, each with the very same message. And like any information which passes through different ears and different hands, what we had been left with did not make any sense at all.

I looked out across the expanse of green and saw a church in the distance, I knew its doors were probably locked today. After all, there was nothing to do in that magnificent sanctuary when Sunday services were over. But, on top of that church, on a tall spire, was a white cross. And in that cross was incredible hope, not for rescue by a supernatural being on some horrible judgment day, but for joyful reunion with the divine which was present now and would surround me forever. I knew it was up to me to move off the horizontal, static, everyday part of that cross. Perhaps as clumsy and homely as the hunchback of Notre Dame, I knew I would climb out of density and live as I was meant to, one with my soul.

I heard a soft whisper, "With all your strength, lift your sight and tears will fall from your eyes and fountains of love will unleash from your heart. Shed your ignorance and look in your heart for that which knows its own lover like no other. Unfasten your joy, release your passion, push away all that holds you back and run toward me with all you have."

I smiled softly through my tears and realized I had again heard the voice of my soul.

Chapter 33

"That's so good, Rick!" Looking up, I barely had time to notice we were no longer sitting on the grass. From underneath me came a powerful force and I was thrust violently into the air. Sparkling blue water streamed from something enormous and I took in a huge breath as we headed down. Eyes wide open with shock, I searched below me in the murky water, unable to believe my mind. Up we went, shooting forward into the sunshine, my arms clutched madly over the back of the beast.

"Daniel! Oh God, Daniel!" I screamed, frantically searching the glittering surface for help. But like a bucking bronco, the animal bent and took me under once again.

"See, first you have to learn a different way to breathe." I heard him clearly in my tortured mind, but he was nowhere to be seen. I gripped harder as my captor took off, rushing through the water.

Suddenly, we broke the surface again and I gasped for air. Through eyes blurred with salt water, I saw pine trees along a distant shore. My mind grasped for what it could and came to the conclusion we must be somewhere in the north. As if that fact could provide me with an answer to my dilemma, I relaxed a little and was promptly submerged again.

"Can't help them unless you learn to breathe differently." Again the little voice spoke directly to my mind.

I silently roared, "What does that mean? Please, just tell me what you mean!"

Abruptly, I sat soaking wet on shore. Shaking water off like an ungainly dog after a bath, I looked around for Daniel. As usual, he was nowhere to be seen. Tall conifers hugged the cold, empty stretch of beach. Abandoned by the tide, driftwood and battered logs lay scattered across the the wet expanse of lonely sand.

Lifting my eyes out over the gray water, I saw a pod of whales off shore. Never before had I seen such a wonderful, wild sight. Astounded by their beauty, I stood up and watched one leviathan breech and then disappear, leaving a dazzling, sun-filled spray of water behind.

"Hi." I turned quickly to see Daniel, definitely dressed for the cold. Clad in jeans, red flannel shirt, boots and gloves, he looked like he'd jumped straight from the pages of an outdoor catalog. On the other hand, I was still sopping wet.

"What in the world was all that about?" My voice sounded angry. I really didn't mean to be irritated with him, but my capacity for dealing with the unexpected had been depleted early in this miraculous day.

"Just wanted you to see," he said. From nowhere, he produced a red and black plaid blanket and held it out to me.

"See what?" I replied, clutching the luscious, soft wool around my shivering body.

"What you have to do," he said as if he expected me to know what he was talking about. Looking a little dismayed, he added, "You know, you don't have to stay cold, unless you really want to."

My trembling had slowed considerably and I answered perfunctorily, "The blanket is working nicely, thank you."

"No," he shook his head. "I mean you don't have to stay that way. Just turn up your energy."

"What?" I didn't have any idea what he was talking about. "How in the world do I do that?"

He looked exasperated and said, "Well, you can start by asking Adam to release some of the energy through your system that you told him he should hang onto when you got scared."

"Oh." I felt silly. After all, I already knew that. It was just that I seemed to forget everything I had learned whenever I got frightened.

"Why do you suppose that is?" he said, reading my mind.

"Because. . . because it seems like the crisis on the outside is real and I have to forget the more subtle things in order to rally and meet it." I knew as soon as I said it that was a ridiculous concept. I had already experienced how limiting that kind of attitude could be.

195

"What do you think happens then?" he asked, knowing I had already come to the appropriate conclusion.

"I know, I know. Social mind has a great opportunity to convince me once again that he's very, very important." I hated that idea. I didn't want social mind to have any control over me ever again.

"Right!" He bent down and picked up a tiny broken shell and asked casually, "So, do you think that's a good thing to have happen?"

"No." I said sheepishly. "When I give him control, I lose abilities, not gain them."

"Yep," he replied, carefully putting the shell back on the sand exactly as he had found it.

Someday, perhaps I would automatically implement what I had learned. It was frustrating to see how quickly social mind could gain the upper hand.

I gazed out to sea and, finding no further sign of the whales asked, "Daniel, what was that all about? What happened back there?"

He began to giggle and said, "I just wanted you to see. So, I thought I'd get your attention."

I felt my irritation come back to the surface like an ugly piece of plastic someone thoughtlessly had tossed into the water. "I don't understand. If I was where I think I was, you could have gotten me killed."

He grinned back at me and said, "Well, see it's like this. People, when they're stuck in their personality self, they're like barnacles on the whale. And the soul, well, it's like the whale you were just riding."

I protested loudly, "Riding! Is that what you would call it!"

Laughing, he replied, "Well, you were trying really hard!"

"Trying to save my life!" I responded adamantly, kicking up some sand with the edge of my shoe.

"Oh Rick, I wouldn't let anything happen to you," he replied, his innocent face completely devoid of sympathy.

That struck me as an extremely inaccurate statement, given what I had experienced today. My mind had been completely shattered, for a start. But, I knew it was good. It had just been incredibly painful at times.

I took in a deep breath of the wonderfully cleansing ocean air and said, "So, why is that important for me to see?"

He had wandered to the edge of the water and crouching down, began to play with some bubbling foam left behind by an unnoticed wave.

"Because you want to try to help people remember who they really are and know what?"

My irritation had ebbed and I walked down to the water. "What?"

Standing up, he looked very serious. "Some of them aren't going to like it at all."

"They aren't?" We moved back quickly as an unexpected rush of water nearly covered our feet.

"Nope." He looked up and reminded me, "You didn't."

He was sure right about that. I felt embarrassed when I considered the spectacular things he had shown me and how I had fought furiously against him most of the way. I was sorry I had been unable to simply embrace what he had wanted to help me experience. "That's true. I apologize."

"That's O.K.," he replied, patting my arm. "Unfortunately, that's the way most people react. See, when you tell them about their soul, some of them don't like the idea that something is more important than who they think they are. They just forget that it's all them. I mean, their soul isn't somebody different telling them what to do, it is them. It's who they really are."

I understood what he was saying. None of us like the idea that we're not as important as we thought we were. "So, they end up feeling like the barnacle when the whale decides to go somewhere. . . kind of powerless."

He was clearly pleased with my understanding. "Yep. But that's a mistake!"

Grateful for the affirmation I added, "Because they're not the barnacle, they're the whale! We're more important than we thought we were, but in a way we had to learn to understand."

"Right!" Daniel was a teacher who was most happy when his student was able to answer the questions himself.

"What did you mean when you said I had to learn how to breathe differently?" He had lost me there. After all, what did breathing have to do with learning about the soul?

"Well," he said adamantly, "if you're going into the realm of the whale, you'd better be able to survive there and not think so much about what's being left behind!"

I nodded in agreement before I realized I didn't really understand what he was telling me. "I'm not quite sure what you mean."

He smiled and answered, "Well, it's just when a person's capsule begins to be challenged, let alone break down, he gets kind of upset."

"Like I did," I confirmed, feeling embarrassed about how difficult it had been to give up what I thought was so important.

"Yep," his voice was reassuring, "See, most people look outside for answers. That's why they end up getting so dependent on keepers and other social minds. They're used to looking into the outside world to tell them all about inside stuff. But that doesn't work at all!"

Of course it wouldn't work. Nothing anybody could tell you could compare to the experience of being out of the capsule. In fact, what most people told you only ended up filling that space with more social mind clutter. I knew what it was like to be free, and that came with a letting go, not an increase of social mind. I said excitedly, "You have to experience being out of the capsule for yourself, like I did!"

"Yep." He paused and we watched a herd of sandpipers dash madly toward the water as it receded and then race speedily for the sand when a little wave swept ashore. He continued, "See, it's kind of like people paddling a boat across the seas, going from place to place, working like crazy to get somewhere to find the answers. But all the while, what they really need to do is get out of the boat and dive into the water and start for the deep."

"Going inward, not outward." That was not common in our culture. People who wanted to spend time with themselves were always suspect. It seemed every time somebody committed an atrocious crime, the first thing others said about him was, "He was always a loner."

But this wasn't about cutting yourself off from other people, it was about knowing that you had an incredible world inside of yourself. Past the concerns of the day, past endless ruminations about other people, your day, your job and your relationships, there was an amazing richness to tap into.

I remembered reading Carl Jung's work about introversion and extroversion. Even those terms evoked judgment in our culture. An introvert was some kind of social incompetent and an extrovert was someone who was wonderfully entertaining to be around. But Jung had described something different. He used the word introvert to describe someone who gained his energy from deep inside himself and an extrovert as the person who gained his energy from people and activities outside of himself. Most of us were definitely in the second category. Our daily life was an exercise in getting energy from the outside so we could go on. With that kind of reliance on the outside, we never even thought to look inside.

The little boy interrupted my thoughts, "It's not a horizontal thing, but a vertical thing. . . you know, a dive, not a paddling!"

I was beginning to understand what he meant. "So, if you're going to dive, you have to learn a different way to breathe."

"Right." The child picked up a long strand of deep gold seaweed and began to snap it back and forth as he went on, "When you jump out of the boat into the inner and away from the outer, well, it's a change in elements, like going from air into water. You're going to be less in personality and more in the realm of spirit. The rules will change."

I knew what most people would think about that idea and said ruefully, "Boy, I can hear social minds all over the place. 'Are you crazy? Stay in the boat! It's dangerous out there.'" Most of us definitely did not like going into the unknown. We wanted to grow, but not change. That was impossible, but we kept trying anyway.

"Right," he said, abruptly dropping his improvised whip. "Not only other personalities, but your own as well."

I took in another deep breath of salt air. "So, there's some panic and uncertainty once you hit the water, once you start looking inside yourself for some answers."

"Yep," he replied, skipping a few yards away. "Confusion, fear, uncertainty. . . and other people probably won't help at all. But see, diving is a solitary thing, not a group thing. If you try to take others with you, they'll just act like buoys, you know, bring you right back up to the surface where you were in the first place."

It was true, if we did decide to go into something unknown, we always wanted to have company. I had done that many times. The next thing you know, you're asking the other person what his experience is like, what he thinks about what you're doing. Then, you get knocked off course when they inevitably have a different idea or want to challenge what you're doing.

Searching the undulating sea, I ventured to say, "You could spend an awfully long time just paddling on the surface, looking for another teacher, another group, another church, another philosophy."

"Yep. Lifetimes. See, once you go into the inner, you can't see where you're going, you don't know how it works and your personality starts yelling like mad for you to go back where it's safe. If you look around, you don't see any other personalities diving. They're all in the boat."

"Because that's what we're taught to do right from the start. Stay where everybody else is." I was really beginning to resent the Greek chorus in everyone's life. It constantly gives a socially correct opinion about everything you do.

"Yep. But, if you stay in the water," he paused and grinned, "you learn to breathe water. . . you learn to draw what you need from the inner, not the outer."

I smiled ruefully and offered, "I bet you never learn that unless you take the plunge, so to speak."

"Nope," he yelled running toward the water. "Personality doesn't want you to learn you can live off the inner stuff! Then it wouldn't have a job, and it wouldn't be able to steal energy from other people and have control over everything."

"But Daniel," I called after him. "I've seen it myself. The inner worlds are so much more beautiful than anything on the surface!"

Suddenly, he was behind me and I jumped when he said, "Yep. But it's scary to begin with, huh?"

"How do you do that?" I muttered. Without waiting for an answer, I offered an example gained from the multiple episodes of terror I had experienced with Daniel today, "To look at it another way, it is kind of like leaping off the ledge into the darkness. You leap before you know how to fly and kind of learn that on the way down!"

"That's a good way to see it," he affirmed. Opening his hand, I was surprised to see a lovely yellow butterfly. "Like if a caterpillar went off the ledge and somehow he becomes a butterfly before he hits the ground."

I watched the magical bit of sunshine flutter merrily away. "Wow, what would happen if the caterpillar refused to give way to the butterfly?"

"Not a pretty sight," he said scrunching up his small face.

I was very familiar with the human character, "Most people aren't going to take a full leap off into nowhere." I had been blessed with the chance to dive straight off a cliff, but most people were not going to volunteer to do the same thing. "You made me do it that way, but isn't it usually different somehow? I mean, doesn't a person have to be ready?"

He heaved a huge sigh. "People are never ready. . . that's the whole problem. If we wait until you're all ready, there will be nothing left!"

"I guess the time for endless meandering is about over, isn't it?" I thought about all the time I had wasted in my life trying to gear up for something uncomfortable. I had grasped at any excuse I could find to avoid doing anything I was afraid of. Nearly everyone I knew was the same way. But we couldn't continue like that. I said sadly, "This second chance is so important because Gaia can't go on like this forever."

"Nope." He looked down the beach as a soft cold wind blew his blond hair back from his face. Then he turned towards me and said brightly, "But see, there's a lot of extra help for you guys right now. The beings from upper heaven are sending lots of helpers into the Earthtime to light the way for you to come home. But it's always got to be free will."

I thought he had said that angels weren't real. "Daniel, I thought you told me it was a waste of time to call out to angels."

"Well it is," he replied quietly. "You have to do your own work to get out of the capsule. But that doesn't mean there isn't wonderful help for you. It's just that you can't sit around expecting something with wings to come along and save you from what you choose to construct for yourself."

I picked up a a gorgeous, soft pink shell and inspected its ridged surface. Carefully, I put it back where I had found it, just as Daniel had done earlier. "So when people say they are talking to angels, seeing angels, is that their imagination?"

"Sometimes," he answered shortly and then added something intriguing. "Sometimes it's a lot more dangerous than that."

"What do you mean?" I geared myself up for another shock of some kind.

He smiled gently as if to comfort me in advance. "Well, you know how you saw the personality self being absorbed back into the soul when the life on Earth ended?"

"Yes," I replied tentatively.

"Well, going back to the soul is always free will, whether you're in the body or out of it." Playfully, he directed the searching arms of a crab in my direction before tenderly setting it down. "Sometimes the personality won't go home and it stays with the Earth."

"Like ghosts, evil spirits, that kind of thing?" I could accept that. After all, just about everyone believed in at least the possibility of haunted houses.

"Well, kind of, sort of, not exactly," he said sitting down on a battered log. "See, a lot of the time, these personalities aren't bad, they're just in the wrong place. And, just like people in bodies, they have the same talents and the same limitations. The problem is, they get tangled up with people's energy who are still living on the Earth."

I decided to become an additional bump on the log and sat beside him, ready for additional information. "Wait a minute! You're not talking about ghosts lingering in a house somewhere. Are you saying these spirits can actually hang out with a living person?"

"Sure," he said matter of factly. He shrugged his shoulders and continued, "See, they start giving advice and talking about stuff they really don't know anything about. Because you guys are so astounded by anything without a body, people usually assume it's an angel or a guide and what he says is valuable. But see, it's usually just a regular personality who doesn't have any more wisdom than he did when he had a body."

People seemed to be obsessed with angels lately. I hadn't really known what to think. It was certainly a romantic idea, but it had seemed too simple to me. "I hear lots of people talk about their guides and angels. Are you telling me these could just be some plumber from Omaha who's getting a lot of attention because he's speaking without a body?"

"Yep."

I looked at him with the wide eyes of new understanding, "No wonder the reports about what they say are often so weird!"

"Yep. Same old social mind, just running around trying to control other people. Except it's a lot easier because your eyes are popping out of your head because the voice doesn't have its own body. The more weird it is, the more people seem to like it."

"But," I protested, "there are other beings, real beings out there! I saw them myself!"

He looked at me reassuringly. "Well, first of all, there is no out there, remember? It's all right here, ready for you to open to it. Rick, your own soul has everything you need. It's what each person should be looking to. That's the most important thing! It's just that there's additional help with the process of going home, that's all."

I felt relieved. "So, we could look at it like our own soul is the only angel we should listen to and go towards."

He smiled and said, "Well, if you insist on calling it an angel, you can. Whatever you want to call it, your own soul is your only way home."

I allowed what he had said to sink in for a moment. It made perfect sense. Why should we look to celestial beings to swoop down and save us? Wasn't that more of the same old mixed up religious teaching? Our own soul was something much more intimate than that. It was what we belonged to. It could provide us with all the love and guidance we needed. I had experienced that first hand.

When I was ready to continue, I asked, "So, what can people expect? I mean, if they're willing to go inward. . . if they're willing to go into the realm of the whale?"

He jumped off the log and began to run in a big circle. Calling out his answer he said, "Well, you know how personality makes all those illusions in its little kingdom of the capsule. In fact, it kind of gets drunk on its creations. It feels like it's the king of its world."

My eyes followed his continuous movement, "Yes, unfortunately, I know that from personal experience. You think the more you achieve financially, socially, physically, the better you are. The more strong and secure you feel. . . except in the middle of the night."

"Right," he said, temporarily out of breath. "Well, when you go into the inner, that begins to break down. You start asking yourself, is that all there is?"

This was familiar territory for me. "When you've got it all and it's still not enough. You still feel empty inside."

"Yep," he replied, holding up a sand polished black stone for my inspection. "The person starts to wake up. They notice that they have a whole bunch of stuff, they're admired, they drive the right car, they look good, and so what?"

I knew this old feeling and I had listened to a thousand clients when they expressed the same thing. "There's really no happiness, no peace inside. You have to beat off the emptiness everyday. . . eat, drink, do drugs, do something to forget the fear."

"Yep. Mostly, people just work harder and do more to try to stop that fear and loneliness." He thought for a moment and said, "After all, holing up in the darkness like a caterpillar in the chrysalis and watching your legs fall off doesn't sound nearly as appealing as competing with the other caterpillars!"

"Well, when you put it that way, it really doesn't." I remembered working frantically, feeling stressed, but much more comfortable than I was when I stopped being busy. Not being busy was a scary thing back in those days. I hadn't wanted to face what I was really feeling inside.

"And see, when the person starts to feel this way, the soul is really happy! But the personality can be really miserable." He smiled and added, "It's hard to convince people that kind of feeling awful is a really good thing."

I stood up and stretched, "Then what happens?"

Copying me, he held his arms up high over his head and said, "Well, people start to face the fact that they aren't their job, they aren't their relationship, they aren't their car. And they want to know, if I'm not those things, what the heck am I?"

Dropping my arms I replied, "The spell of those illusions in the capsule is broken!"

"Right."

I temporarily took on the role of my teacher, "And all the things you used to draw your identity from, like how much you make and how you look and who you know and what trip you're going to be able to take, all that starts to not matter so much. You're left wondering just who am I?"

"Yep. Then, the person starts to let go of the stuff he used to think of as him. Once he knows it isn't him, he doesn't want to spend his time working so hard to keep it all. The old things don't seem nearly as important as figuring out who he is."

I considered for a moment how my own friends were going to react when I began to change my life in accordance with what I had learned today. I sighed and said, "That's when all the other personalities really get upset!"

Daniel took a few steps back and pushed his toes deep into the wet sand before saying, "The person can't really tell people what he's feeling. It doesn't make much sense to him yet. All he knows is he's not the stuff on the outside. The kingdom of the capsule is not all there is."

"So, other people start sending him to people like I used to be. . . counselors, doctors, that kind of thing. To get him fixed, back the way he used to be. A good, solid, productive citizen."

All of our mental health standards had to do with how well the person was able to function in his societally determined roles. Was he able to perform well at work? Did he dress within standard norms? Was he able to set responsible goals and fulfill them adequately? Did he get along well with others? As soon as the person got back in line, we were happy.

The little boy surveyed my increasing dismay at the role I had played in keeping others trapped in social mind. Then he said, "Right back in the capsule. People don't like somebody breaking out. It makes them nervous. They react by trying to get him to stop. If that doesn't work, they harden up the walls of their own capsule, call the other person selfish, or sick, or some other bad name."

"But that's really just their social mind getting its power threatened!" I had always hated anything that had to do with imprisonment. The idea that I could become trapped, unable to make my own choices and not allowed to live in my own way had motivated me to pursue an independent career. I had deliberately stayed well away from corporate life because I had a definite fear of being under someone else's thumb. But the whole time, I had my own slave owner inside. And like any plantation prince, mine didn't want me to know there was any possibility of true freedom.

"Right." He watched me for a moment before continuing, "And you know what? Sometimes the person will get so mixed up, he'll go back to the old way of looking at it, just to please the other people. That's really sad and his Adam sometimes will just think that lifetime doesn't have any purpose any more. Next thing you know, the body starts breaking down. . . illness, accidents, severe depression, withering up."

I had tears in my eyes as I thought of the incredible strength of bound people everywhere who had broken their chains and bolted for freedom. I said quietly, "But, some people will find the courage to keep going."

"Yep." He offered me another shell to look at. Although it was no longer occupied, clearly it had once been some creature's shelter. I wondered if that life had outgrown this container and gone in search of another one. Did it have more freedom to move than we allowed ourselves?

Daniel interrupted my thoughts with a statement of hope, "Sometimes a person gets really determined and goes forward and starts pushing on the walls of the capsule really hard."

"And that's wonderful!" What an incredible day of liberation that would be for any person who was strong enough to claim what should be his. The little boy surprised me with his reply.

"Well, kind of, sort of, not exactly. See, the first thing that happens to the capsule when it begins to actually break down is that personality sees the end of the kingdom and gets super upset."

I should have known it couldn't be that simple. "Kind of like death throes?"

"Yep." Temporarily distracted by a rowdy seagull screaming overhead, Daniel turned his back to me and then continued, "So it sends up awful anxiety. Sometimes the person starts running around being really frantic. He wants to know, if his life isn't going to be what he thought it was, then what is it going to be? He wants to know that right now. And he wants to know exactly."

I walked around to face him, "And that's impossible to know because he hasn't gone far enough yet to really see anything for himself. He's just starting to break free."

"Right," he said, catching a white feather drifting on the breeze. "He can't really go back, 'cause once you see the kingdom is false, well, you can't just forget about that."

"So, that's a pretty miserable stage," I said, inspecting the delicate gray edges on this remnant of bird attire.

He shrugged his small shoulders and replied, "Sometimes. People can have lots of symptoms, be really scared, get more depressed, uncertain."

From within me, the answer from social mind found its well practiced pathway and was immediately available. "And other personalities say, 'Ah ha, I told you not to go that direction. See how unhappy you are!'"

"Yep," he nodded. "The other social minds are really, really pleased because their people are never going to challenge that part of themselves after watching somebody else's misery."

I said softly, "But the soul is very happy with the person's progress."

His voice softened, "The soul is singing with joy as the pieces of the capsule fall away. It keeps sending love and encouragement and tells the person that the way out of all that pain is to keep going, to keep letting the capsule break apart."

But I knew human nature very well. "Some people won't go any farther. They'll get scared by the pain and never find what's beyond that stage, right?"

"Yep." Using the tone of a parent correcting a wayward child, he pronounced, "That's enough. Stop right here and just sit down." He lifted his hands in an attitude of supplication and said, "Then they're stuck, afraid to go forward and afraid to go back. The realm of the whale is unknown and

206

it's proven to be pretty painful so far, but the kingdom of the capsule has no meaning any more."

Again, I watched the sandpipers race away from the water, then turn in tandem and run as fast as they could straight into it again. Human behavior was actually quite similar. "So, they run around trying to get somebody outside to fix that pain. A new teacher, counselor, religion, anything."

"I'm afraid so," he replied. "See, if they would just keep going forward, watch for the subtlety of the soul, be quiet, take the time to ask questions and listen inside for the answers, well, things would be a whole lot different."

I shook my head, "We're awfully set on immediate relief, immediate gratification. That's what our culture was all about. How to do something, get something, be something as fast as possible." But, now I could understand much better why it was like that. With social mind continually increasing in power and ready to rob anyone whenever possible, we all had to run as fast as we could just to keep up.

The little boy nodded in agreement, "Just a tool of social mind to fool you and keep the power."

My teeth ground with frustration, "It doesn't want you to find out that all of this is just a birthing process, a re-emergence into your larger self. Once you really let it all go, there is no more pain."

"Right." Daniel paused a long while. When he continued, his voice was achingly gentle and filled with love. "You don't need to live in your dark little container. You don't need to remain trapped and lost and alone. You don't need to try to find freedom from your pain by going after substances, people and things that will divert you from it. You don't have to stay agitated and confused.

"But, if you really want your freedom, you have to do something that's really different from what most people would ever do. Instead of hanging on as hard as you can, you have to let fall away and die what you think is you. And you will find when that dies away, you are so much more than what has been lost!"

My eyes filled again at the irony of it all. "That's the paradox. What seems like the end of everything, is really the beginning of everything. And you don't disappear. After all, I'm still here!"

"Yep," he said. "Your feet will remain on Gaia, but it's no longer just ground, but the mother from upper heaven in whose arms you rest. Spirit is everywhere! It's who you are, wherever you are and whatever you do."

My face was wet with tears and salt spray, cousins from the same source. "And we've come so far. Our souls have been lost such a long, long time. Now we have the real chance to make it all the way home."

"You should honor yourselves for how far you've come," he said gently. "After all, it's been a long, treacherous journey."

I gathered myself together and focused on the boundless hope for mankind I had seen in the faces of the souls. "So, if people will go through that process you just described, they can find their way out of the capsule!"

Brightly he replied, "Well, they don't have to suffer like that! Suffering isn't an essential part of spiritual growth. We see lots of people all over your Earth doing terrible things to themselves in the name of spirit. You know, beating themselves, fasting, living in awful conditions and staying just as rigidly in social mind as the person who lives in luxury. It's not suffering that does the trick, it's letting go. You only suffer to the degree that you refuse to let go."

I smiled as I remembered how miraculously full I had been when I had allowed room for my soul. Nothing could ever compare to that feeling. "And when you let go, the soul can come flowing in."

Making room was only a sacrifice on the level of social mind. Like ripping the wrapping paper from a Christmas present is a loss, what's inside the box is so much more! While we were stuck, unable to face giving up what we could see, we never got to the good stuff. If we wouldn't agree to something changing, we would never have room for anything different to come in. "Just like you told me, the soul can only enter to the exact degree that you make room for it to do so."

"Yep." His face beamed with the possibilities, "And when the heart opens, people can give and receive those energies of love and even use these energies to transform everything they touch. The heart opening up is like your nose opening to receive air. See, love is the thing that fuels life in all the realms."

My heart was filled with hope for all of us. "And we can make a conscious commitment to bring those soul energies through ourselves and right into the Earth!"

Again his voice grew soft and full of love, "You have all crawled forth from the same place, you have been lost for the same time, you have suffered in the same way and you belong to the same home. Each person, no matter how unlikable their personality capsule might be, shares the same experience. Once your heart is opened, when you encounter another person and your eyes meet, you will see the light of spirit shining within them. You will see right past the clothes of form."

He continued, "Once your heart is opened, you experience first hand, the reality of your enormous true nature! You can act from the ground of who you really are and who that other person really is, no matter what is happening at a personality level."

It was so elegantly simple and I exclaimed, "We can become conscious, aware and constantly in love! We actually begin to replace all the thick energy and darkness of density with love and light of the highest quality from the soul."

He nodded in affirmation, "You can pour fresh and clean sparkling water into a bucket filled with brown, stagnated water. The more clear and sparkling energy you pour into the dark water, the lighter and lighter the water becomes. After a while it's all clear and beautiful again."

"Daniel, it's so beautiful!" I said, happiness sweeping through me. "It's so miraculous. . . and it's been right here all along!"

The little boy stood now in front of me. His chest began to shimmer and glow beneath his red shirt and that light grew and grew until radiant beams of violet, silver and gold began to skip out across the lonely beach. Taking my hand, his sparkling blue eyes reflected the truth of forever.

Ever so gently, his whisper caressed my deepest heart, "Past the wounds of childhood, past the fallen dreams and the broken families, through the hurt and the loss and the agony only the night ever hears, is a waiting soul. Patient, permanent, abundant, it opens its infinite heart and asks only one thing of you. . . 'Remember who it is you really are.'"

With a soft little smile, he disappeared.

Chapter 34

I heard it first. "Ladies and Gentlemen, we will be landing in London in approximately thirty minutes. Please begin to place your belongings back in the overhead storage compartments. The flight attendants will assist you if needed. . ."

I opened my eyes. There it all was. . . the 747, the passengers, my tray table with its drink. "Daniel." His name came from my mouth like a prayer, "Daniel?"

"Can I help you, Sir?" A kind face appeared past the sunny voice.

"Well, I'm not sure. I'm a little confused right now." I stumbled over my words while looking up and down the aisle for my teacher.

"I bet you had a good sleep. It's pretty uncommon to be next to an empty seat on a transatlantic flight! Better get ready to land. We're almost there." With that, she walked away.

"Daniel, this isn't funny," I muttered. "Where are you?" Held back by the worried looks coming from the woman across the aisle, I stopped talking. Where had he gone this time? I knew perfectly well, I hadn't been alone on this flight, despite what the attendant had said. My heart was different. I could feel it, turning unencumbered, filled with love.

Over the stir of passengers anticipating an end to the long flight, I heard the landing gear thud into place. The lights of the old city reached up to greet us and I wondered if anyone else realized what I knew now. How was I going to explain all of this to anyone? An unspoken shout reverberated in my head, "It's not really the way it seems to be!"

We arrived at the gate and I dutifully followed the rest of the people off the aircraft. Searching constantly, I could find no sign of the child. Stepping out into the soft drizzle that is London's constant companion, I hailed a cab.

Hoping to see Daniel just once more, I looked across the buzzing confusion of people and cars. Finding nothing, I climbed inside and let myself sink back into the seat.

"Where to?" the driver asked.

"Hilton on Park Lane," I answered quietly.

The rain was harder now, sending little rivers down the windows and turning the world outside into a blur of colors. Closing my eyes for a moment, I released the breath held in the ache within my heart. I thought about how much Daniel had given me in such a short time; I had never even had the chance to thank him.

My hands rested over my awakened heart and I gratefully remembered all I had experienced. Lost in my feelings for a minute, I suddenly realized the vehicle had not moved. Slowly opening my eyes, I was astounded to find the little boy sitting behind the steering wheel. Turning, he grinned and said, "Now what do you want to do?" He looked over at me, confident I would have an answer.

"Daniel! Daniel, thank God you're here!" I cried, leaning forward in my seat to touch his shoulder.

"Of course I'm here!" he replied brightly. "Where else would I be?"

I looked back at him in amazement and reminded him, "You do have a habit of disappearing!"

"Only when you don't know how to look," he giggled.

"Are you trying to tell me you don't go anywhere?" I shook my head in disbelief. "It's just me that sometimes can't see you?"

The familiar peals of laughter rang out in the cab. Tears began to fall down his sweet face with the humor of it all as he said, "Silly, of course I don't go anywhere!"

Despite everything he had taught me, that thought had never occurred to me. Of course he didn't go anywhere, that was the point he had tried to get through my head from the beginning. There is truly no separation except that which we create ourselves.

The unnerving prospect of a little boy driving through the streets of London, intruded into my consciousness, "Wait a minute! Daniel, are you going to drive? Where are we going?"

"That's up to you." His little face showed a determination not to make things easy for me.

211

"I don't know what to say." I struggled for a moment with the possibilities. All I could think of was not allowing him to drive. "Where do we go from here?"

He looked a little exasperated and said, "Well, you can go back or you can go forward. . . that's not too hard to figure out."

A tremendous resolve exploded in my heart, "Of course I don't want to go back! I want to keep going forever!"

"Are you sure?" He said with a challenge in his voice as he turned his back to me.

"Of course I'm sure!" I said, as a new thought penetrated my mind. "You have more to teach me, don't you?" Please let that be true, I pleaded silently.

I wanted to continue to grow, to reach beyond my capsule, to learn to be free from it forever. I wanted to learn to hear the voice of my soul all the time and bask its love without interruption. I wanted to bring those energies to Gaia as an offering to her boundless patience. And my soul community, what was my affiliation? I needed to learn about what I had sensed beyond Upper Heaven. . . where had the voice come from? And . . . just who was Daniel?

"Lot's more!" he replied happily.

The two words liberated my heart and I was overwhelmed with a wave of courage, "Well then, let's get to it!"

I could see the little boy in the overhead mirror and a smile crossed his face like the rising sun. Voice full of admiration he said softly, "I told them you would want to do that. . . just checking!"

With that, the vehicle disappeared and we sped, parting glimmering seas of silver light, straight for my soul. And again, there was no "Rick," but only the bountiful, ecstatic love of everything that is. Together, we looked out across the Earth and saw human beings everywhere, trapped inside their lonely capsules. And our heart wept tears of grief for their choices to remain separate and frightened. And with all the longing the heavens held, we sent out the cries of a million years, "Do not be afraid, for we are with you always."

But even as people remained closed, the soul patiently surrounded each one and floated beautifully around them, a diaphanous, glistening, love-filled being of wondrous, pulsing energy. And sometimes, that soul was allowed to make its way into the heart, and then that heart would begin to turn, spinning with glorious, waterfalls of light. When it did, everything around it would begin to awaken and heal, shrugging off its mottled prison and searching for its deepest desire.

And Gaia breathed beneath me and I saw her heart wheel sending spectacular torrents of love through all creation. I heard her singing to her children and whispering encouragement to each one. And from her noble trees and mystic mountains, from the delicate flowers swaying in a morning field, in the voice of the wind and the cry of a bird, she had forever called the same message, "Keep going. . . do not be afraid. . . never give up. . . your home is within sight. . . only open your heart once more."

THE END

DANIEL IS REAL!

In 1991, Daniel began to provide the astounding information you have read about in *Losing Your Mind*. Although he has never had a body on Earth, he has an intimate understanding of humanity's pain and continues to offer teaching dedicated to helping us to personally reach the wisdom and boundless love of our own soul. His work is filled with intelligence, compassion and patience before only dreamed of by those in his audience.

The Foundation for Spiritual Training was formed to provide continuing access to Daniel's teaching and offers the following opportunities for you to personally experience this great teacher.

INTRODUCTORY VIDEO

Watch as Daniel speaks directly through Karen Alexander. Witness the incredible love which has touched countless lives as he teaches us how we can find our way out of life's confusion and pain. Go beyond what you have already learned in this book and continue to grow toward liberation from the capsule which you have been trapped in from your earliest days on Earth. See for yourself what can happen when you decide to challenge the conventional ideas which have led to the human predicament.

DANIEL'S JOURNAL

You don't have to wait for the next book to receive Daniel's latest teaching! Published quarterly, this beautifully written journal contains priceless information to guide you in your journey home to the soul. Daniel's work is filled with practical, humorous and enlightening messages which directly address the human quest for liberation.

RETREAT OPPORTUNITIES WITH DANIEL

Gathering people from all over the country, Daniel's retreats have become legendary. In an atmosphere of utmost safety and boundless love, he offers a three day experience which can be dramatically powerful. Receive personal instruction from this generous teacher about how you can enhance your life beyond your wildest expectations. Join with others as we break free of our limitations and pain and head toward home.

For a list of retreat dates and locations, and a registration packet, please contact:

The Foundation for Spiritual Training
1-800-359-4492

AUDIO RECORDINGS OF DANIEL'S TEACHING

As Daniel continues to speak to groups, a library of audio tapes has grown. These tapes allow you to listen to Daniel's loving voice as he presents invaluable help designed to assist you in your own spiritual work.

Please request a free complete catalog from the Foundation for Spiritual Training.

"Movement Toward Spirit"

Learn how your personality separates you from the energy, wisdom and knowledge of your own soul. You can break free of the density and liberate the passion which will propel you home. An enlightening and encouraging tape that describes what you can expect as you move toward spirit.

"Signposts Along the Spiritual Path"

Your soul has infinite passion for bringing you home. This inspiring tape shows you what the steps on the spiritual path can be and teaches you how you can receive all the love and wisdom waiting for you.

"The Enemy in Your Midst"

Daniel speaks extensively about social mind, its tricks, traps and methods for keeping you caught in the capsule and separated from your soul. Learn to recognize when your own social mind has you in its clutches and how to free yourself from its grip. This tape can also be invaluable in healing relationships that seem hopelessly conflicted.

GUIDED HYPNOSIS TAPES

Written by Karen Alexander and recorded by Rick Boyes, these audio tapes offer an opportunity to travel into your own inner realms.

"At the Very Center"

At your core lies a limitless wellspring of wisdom and energy. This tape provides you with an opportunity to learn to access what some would call your Highest Self.

"Creating Spiritual Protection"

Your own natural energy can be harnessed to protect you from the unwanted negativity of other people, as well as that which exists on an energy level. Learn a specific technique to keep yourself clear of everything but the highest energies.

"Finding the Child Within"

Daniel has taught the inner child within each of us represents the place where the soul first touched your lifetime. This Divine Child can be incredibly valuable in your quest to reach that soul. Using a startlingly different approach which speaks directly to your inner child, this is an extremely powerful tape. A healing experience, this tape can save you much wasted time and frustration in your process of internal change.

HOME STUDY COURSE: PART I

For the past few years, Daniel has led a select group of people through a dramatic process of spiritual, intellectual and emotional change. What can only be called "personal miracles" have astounded all who have participated.

Now you have the opportunity to experience that same level of teaching in your own home. Comprised of one video tape, six audio tapes and written materials, you can begin your own process of personal liberation from the capsule and the interference of social mind.

You will learn specific techniques which will open your mind and heart beyond their current capacity. Directly experience the person you are outside the confines of the physical body. Learn how to heal personal pain and the relationships which are now filled with hurt.

Most importantly, begin to know the wishes of your own soul.

Please contact The Foundation for Spiritual Training for availability.

Ordering Information

All Audio Tapes $7.00 (Plus $1.00 S/H per tape)
Introductory Video Tape $20.00 (Plus $2 S/H per tape)
Daniel's Journal $30.00 annual subscription
Home Study Course: Part 1 $90.00 (Plus $5 S/H per course)
(Idaho Residents add 5% sales tax on product total before adding shipping costs)

Visa/Mastercard orders call 1-800-359-4492 or Fax to 208-345-1927

Make checks payable to:
Foundation for Spiritual Training
967 Parkcenter Blvd., Suite 306
Boise, Idaho 83706-6700

COMING SOON!

AN ANCIENT WHISPER:
The Erotic Life of the Soul
by Karen Alexander and Rick Boyes

In a miraculous adventure, Daniel propels Rick straight into the heart of his soul and opens this spectacular experience to human beings for the first time. Travel straight into the embrace of the one who has loved you across time. Know what it is like to fill ecstatically with the energies of your ulitmate lover.

What is life like from the perspective of the soul? What company does it keep? What does it do with the experiences it has gathered from your lifetimes on Earth? What is life like after death and before the next lifetime? What is the evolutionary journey of the soul really like? What does your own soul want you to do with this lifetime?

In this powerful, multi-dimensional thriller, escape from the entrapment of the ordinary senses and look into the realm from which you came. . . know at last where you are going. . . know first hand who waits for you with a passion unknown on Earth.

> *"In one corner of the vast plain of darkness, a fire sends up its mystical tribute to the stars in a burst of crimson and orange. Tonight, only one person stands watching, always careful to worship both the heavens and the Earth.*
>
> *And there are eyes everywhere. Filled with an immeasurable love, they watch the ones on Earth for they are treasured without exception. And they know the meaning and purpose of each lifetime, having been present through every birth and death and all that came between. In the silence, they whisper their passion for those they made and wait with limitless patience for the time when they will return home."*

An Ancient Whisper
©Windover Press 1995

THE AUTHORS

Long before the New Age movement began, **Karen Alexander** was receiving information from the spiritual realm. As a child, she astounded people by reporting visits from "people without bodies" who offered clear pictures of life beyond Earth. She learned to hide her abilities going on to academic achievement at the University of California. She earned two Master's degrees with high honors and built a successful counseling practice, specializing in survivor's of childhood trauma.

Rick Boyes graduated from Idaho State University with high honors and began a successful private counseling practice specializing in survivors of sexual abuse and eating disorders. His work changed dramatically when he became a Certified Clinical Hypnotherapist and began to encounter the spiritual dimension directly from his clients in trance. His mind already stretched well beyond his "normal American upbringing," life took a radical flight far beyond his greatest imaginings when he met Karen. Guided by her clear vision, they began to travel through the spiritual dimension, gathering information and experiences which far exceed anything known before. Uniquely grounded in traditional University training, they are able to present their story with honor, grace and intelligence.

Together, Rick and Karen have formed The Foundation for Spiritual Training which provides teaching for those who wish to take life's most exciting adventure. . . the journey straight into the arms of the soul!